D1488416

Secret Journeys

Secret Journeys

Theory and Practice in Reading Dickens

Nicholas H. Morgan

Rutherford • Madison • Teaneck
Fairleigh Dickinson University Press
London and Toronto: Associated University Presses

Associated University Presses
440 Forsgate Drive
Cranbury, NJ 08512

Associated University Presses
25 Sicilian Avenue
London WC1A 2QH, England

Associated University Presses
P.O. Box 39, Clarkson Pstl. Stn.
Mississauga, Ontario,
LSJ 3X9 Canada

The paper used in this publication meets the requirements
of the American National Standard for Permanence of Paper
for Printed Library Materials Z39.48–1984.

Library of Congress Cataloging Data
Morgan, Nicholas H., 1953–
    Secret journeys: theory and practice in reading Dickens /
Nicholas H. Morgan.
        p.   cm.
    Includes bibliographical references and index.
    ISBN 0–8386–3447–8 (alk. paper)
    1. Dickens, Charles, 1812–1870—Criticism and interpretation.
2. Reader-response criticism. I. Title.
PR4592.R36M67   1992
832'.8—dc20   91-55022
                                                          CIP

For Marjie, Sarah, and Eric,

who pulled for this too.

Betsey Trotwood
David Copperfield

Contents

Preface

He led them down dank ways,
over grey Ocean tides, the Snowy Rock,
past shores of Dream and narrows of the sunset,
in swift flight to where the Dead inhabit
wastes of asphodel at the world's end.
Homer, Odyssey 11.10–14*

I have been chasing that will-o'-the-wisp, that insubstantial presence, that fictive literary giant Charles Dickens for nearly fifteen years, first in the mind and now, for the third time, on paper. It was not until midjourney that I realized that I was chasing not a thing but a process, and began to develop a theory of criticism that was first of all a theory of reading.

In part a response to students who seemed to require more and more prodding to share my joy and excitement about nineteenth-century literature, this theoretical journey has always had a practical aspect to it. In the classroom, bringing the late twentieth-century student mind into a happy state of fusion with the Victorian demands an energy at least symbolically akin to that needed by the physicists in their elusive work.

But I have sought also to bring the critical debate into more useful areas of discussion than the postmodernist agenda has permitted of late. As that new form of (an old) radical skepticism known as "free play" or "textuality" has undercut the philosophical ground for literary criticism, critics have become more and more uncertain about their roles and indeed their subjects. I believe that critics are servants; their works do not have the same status as those that they describe. Once a philosophical positioning has been achieved, and presuppositions have been frankly disclosed, critical study should seek to explicate and to provide cultural contexts for the primary works of art it takes in hand. Thus I offer in the present work both a theoretical essay and extended discussions of four of Dickens's works.

Dickens's novels form a multifaceted canon with strong family resem-

---

*Odyssey, trans. Robert Fitzgerald (New York: Doubleday & Co., 1961), bk. 24.

blances (and differences) among its members. My method encompasses such a rich profusion by emphasizing not an essence behind the works but rather the concrete experience of reading them—from a particular perspective. I follow primarily three aspects of the canon through several novels: the dialectic between "fancy" and "authority," the psychology of symbol and memory, and the relationship between narrator and reader. I apply my theoretically grounded, pluralistic method of reading Dickens to *The Old Curiosity Shop, David Copperfield, Little Dorrit,* and *Great Expectations.*

In *The Old Curiosity Shop* the narrator explicitly places Little Nell "in a kind of allegory." Mr. Quilp and Little Nell together live and die at opposite ends of a symbolic chain of desire. Where does that leave us, the readers? Perhaps searching for some middle ground, neither demonic nor otherworldly, which we may inhabit in worldly peace.

David Copperfield becomes for me a specific example that illustrates certain tensions inherent in the first-person narrative form. David attempts to dig up the secrets of his soul, an archaeology. He also works, however, toward a teleology, a comforting, coherent explanation of what his life means. As readers, we must carry out our own psychological investigations before we choose sides in this deeply personal struggle.

Little Dorrit portrays nineteenth-century England as a "jumble sale" of isolated, lonely individuals. Arthur's gloomy childhood under his mother's austere rule made vital his self-assertion in his own private world of fancy. Both Arthur and the reader find that, as adults, escape and imprisonment do not differ as markedly as would first appear when one lives in a self-constructed world of fancy's making.

For a final example, I turn to *Great Expectations,* a first-person narrative that both reveals and conceals much. Pip unknowingly lets slip matters that he wishes to keep secret; the tension between disclosure and concealment forces readers to provide their own connections when Pip does not. If we are willing, we readers will find the unleashing of Pip's childhood ghosts an opportune time for the reexamination of our own.

In conclusion, I suggest some of the patterns that emerge from a journey through the Dickensian universe from a particular reader's viewpoint, while avoiding the temptation to unlock secret doors leading to the revelation of central Dickensian mysteries.

I have received an extraordinary amount of help from many colleagues for a critical journey that has taken so long to complete. That those to whom I have gone again and again for aid have always responded warmly and helpfully is a source of both deep gratitude and astonishment for me. Paul Armstrong, Ralph Cohen, Emory Elliott, Don Hirsch, Dudley Johnson, Walt Litz, Austin Quigley, Edgar Shannon, and Judith Wilt have all sustained me in my circuitous travels, and I am grateful. Thanks also to Dorothy Burd and Janet Anderson, who helped with preparation of the manuscript and provided lively commentary, often simultaneously.

In addition, Dickensian scholars whose work I have returned to again and again bear special mention beyond a mere bibliographical entry. They include Philip Collins, Fred Kaplan, and Alexander Welsh, as well as those of another age, like G. K. Chesterton, whose work seems always fresh, cranky, and invigorating.

Finally, my wife, Marjorie, has borne with the protracted and sometimes painful processes of academic production with patience and perspicacity. For that she deserves all plaudits. She has given me hope.

Secret Journeys

Daniel Peggotty
David Copperfield

1
Critical Issues

Then I addressed the blurred and breathless dead,
vowing to slaughter my best heifer for them
before she calved, at home in Ithaka,
and burn the choice bits on the altar fire;
as for Teiresias, I swore to sacrifice
a black lamb, handsomest of all our flock.
Thus to assuage the nations of the dead
I pledged these rites, then slashed the lamb and
   ewe,
letting their black blood stream into the wellpit.
Now the souls gathered, stirring out of Erebos,
brides and young men, and men grown old in pain,
and tender girls whose hearts were new to grief;
many were there, too, torn by brazen lanceheads,
battle-slain, bearing still their bloody gear.
From every side they came and sought the pit
with rustling cries; and I grew sick with fear.

Homer, *Odyssey* 11.29–44

i

Reading is a journey. When we read, we travel in a multitude of imagined directions—deeper into ourselves, into other places and times, into other spheres of subjectivity—and often all of these at once. In this sense, a text is a form of latent communication, not "switched on" until it is picked up by the reader and engaged. All of its delights and perils ultimately spring from this source, a source within ourselves.

Each act of reading is, then, a specific journey to anywhere undertaken by a unique, "situated" reader. Ancient Troy, or twentieth-century

Dublin, a whaling ship, the Dakotas, a gloomy Danish castle, the inner circles of Hell, a Russian village—or, as in the present case, Victorian England and other nineteenth-century locales—are a few examples from many. Readers, too, are infinitely various. When we generalize ("critics," "readers," "modern readers," or "twentieth-century critics") we lose track of what is essentially theirs: their own particular starting points.

As a journey, reading is often hazardous. Unfamiliar language, unpleasant experiences, and personalities, horrors, places, and times we might rather not explore more deeply, secrets we might rather not know, await us. The work of enlivening this communication can be arduous and risky. It is at least not voyeuristic, however, because of the work we ourselves do in bringing a text to life. We *are* participants. Unlike its rival media—television, film—the book makes us earn our knowledge of other lives and secret places.

Our active status comes with the picking up of the book, with the initial caresses of our eyes on the page, with the forming of that intimate relationship between ourselves and the revealing words the text (often reluctantly) yields up to us.

Many of the difficulties that arise in this relationship have to do with our particular "situatedness" in a place in time and the corresponding "location" of the text.[1] Just as we must reside, firmly rooted, in a particular cultural milieu, so too does the text spring from a particular author similarly situated. When communication occurs, then, it often involves the touching of hands across a chasm of subjective difference—perilous, uncertain, and sometimes unsuccessful. As readers, we have limited local perspectives, just as the text does. When we read a novel, for example, we bring the literary communication to life on partial information. As the Henry James critic Paul Armstrong has noted, "Even in everyday experiences, . . . we know the world by composing wholes from a limited point of view, which leaves some things hidden and indeterminate. All understanding has its own particular perspective on the world and is guided by a certain set of assumptions and expectations. For the novelist, then, the secret of realistic representation is to arrange the aspects and indeterminacies in the work so as to persuade the reader to bring its world to life by remembering his or her own everyday practices of understanding—understanding that is similarly perspectival, never fully determinate, and actively compositional."[2]

What is the role of the critic in this "compositional" work? I believe the critic can best function as a guide, precisely because the journey is an arduous one, to the strange times and places readers may encounter in their travels. The critic's principal duty is to illumine and enliven readers' encounter with the text. In this journey into the dark, the critic carries a lamp.[3]

The critic's job is especially important when the culture and language of another era is sufficiently distant from our own that misunderstandings may easily arise. Such is the case with nineteenth-century works in general and Dickens in particular. Indeed, for Dickens, just as for other writers who loom so large in our cultural history, a special complication arises beyond the usual ones. Dickens's works are dangerous because of their distance from us in many ways. They are also dangerous, however, because of their familiarity. Their status as cultural icons gives readers a cliché-ridden, piecemeal knowledge of them before even beginning to read, and such knowledge is necessarily distorting. Thus, a Dickens critic must seek to make these famous works at once newly familiar and newly strange.

With these precautionary words arming me, I am almost ready to turn to the nineteenth century and to the Dickensian journeys that await us. So complex a journey should not be undertaken, however, without a good working knowledge of the map to be used and of the terrain that map attempts to describe. I need to make clear, in short, the philosophical ground on which I stand before we take our first steps together.

To provoke the necessary questions to delineate that ground, I will not leap all the way back to the Victorian period with my first step, but halfway, and to a simpler textual form than the "baggy monsters," as Henry James called them, of the Victorian era.[4] A fairy-tale collection of the early years of this century will provide a simpler way to ask the necessary theoretical questions.

ii

In 1915, then, the English Leicester Galleries approached the French artist and illustrator Edmund Dulac with a proposal to illustrate a collection of Russian fairy tales. The proposal paralleled the one that launched young Charles Dickens's career. *Pickwick Papers* began as a series of short pieces to accompany sporting scenes to be drawn by a well-known artist of the period, Robert Seymour. For his part, Dulac quickly expanded his project to include fairy stories from each of the Allied nations, more or less, and thus the final version included tales from Russia, England, Belgium, Italy, France, Ireland, Serbia, Japan, and China.[5] It was an extraordinary idea in several ways, this book of children's tales selected in part because of an adult war. The book looked backward to the Victorian period just past, which witnessed the apotheosis of childhood as a separate, inviolate state of innocence.[6] At the same time, Dulac's collection looks ahead, with its sanguinary principles of inclusion, to a twentieth century that was to be utterly transformed by that first war and by the wars that came after.[7] In many ways, our world of the late twentieth century would simply be no longer recognizable to a nineteenth-century observer, and the wars of our era are in large part a cause.

The first piece in the collection, a Russian tale with the ungainly title of "Snegorotchka," tells the bittersweet story of an old childless couple that sneaks out one day to make a snow person, just as the children of their village do in play. The snow child comes to life and delights the couple and the other children with her winsome ways for an entire winter, only to melt away into nothing in the spring. In Dulac's illustration, the snow child is barely visible against the snow background from which she has come; only her face is pink and full of life. The artist's depiction thus clearly signals the instability of this snow creature, even as fairy-tale traditions suggest perhaps two possible outcomes. Either the child will melt forever, or will melt in the spring only to reappear each winter. The latter possibility would involve the transforming power of love, which is so often the agent of happy endings in fairy tales. In this case, however, the love of the old folks is not strong enough, and Snegorotchka is gone forever.[8]

To a literary critic in the late twentieth century the tale, the collection and the strange nature of its creation inevitably suggest questions that delineate the nature of the postmodernist search for appropriate ways to respond to the literature of the past. Even so apparently simple a genre as the fairy tale reveals complexities on closer inspection, especially a collection of tales as oddly chosen as the current one. The theme of "Snegorotchka" at an immediate level is the discovery and loss of love. Why does the adventure befall an old, childless couple? The question answers itself, until we generalize it and ask why so many of the fairy tales in Dulac's collection invoke a similar theme. Is Dulac particularly sensitive to the loss of innocence as his world sinks into war? Does he have an unusual sensitivity to his extraordinary historical position, as the Victorian period and its Edwardian aftermath are dying in the brutal realities of the twentieth century?

Answers to these questions of intention and meaning can come from a study of the genre of the fairy tale, or even the children's book (i.e., the loss of innocence is a widespread theme). They can come from studies of Dulac's life (what we make, for example, of his tendency to idealize his mistress-wife's face in many of his illustrations of innocence and beauty). Or they might come from cultural studies that would tell us what the artistic and social dialogue about innocence and experience was as World War I ground on.

Another set of questions emerges if we go back to the tale itself. In several places, the text takes up the fear that the old people have that Snegorotchka is only a dream, a fiction. And she herself delights the children by creating fictions—castles and fairy towns made of the snow from whence she came. Is all this simply foreshadowing of her own "fictional" state and ultimate dissolution? Or is it something more: a way of evoking the issues of reality and fiction and the relationship that wish-fulfillment forges between them? Is it a self-reflexive piece that is finally about fiction itself? One group of critics has argued powerfully that all fiction is (in more complex ways, to be sure) self-reflexive.[9] Does the inherent formalism of this argument necessarily limit the answer to an affirmation of a formalist stance? In other words, if we look for those parts of fiction that announce their fictive qualities, are we at the heart of the matter, or have we only found out something relatively obvious about the nature of fiction and indeed of language?

These are questions that ultimately will be begged if we refer back to the text for their adjudication. We are still in the realm of meaning because we are analyzing communication, which must be construed as meaningful by definition. We have identified the text, and the author (and his cultural milieu) as possible sources of confirmation or negation of the questions that arise from reading. We can also identify a third broad field of meaning: the reader. But the meaning of this meaning must be developed at some length.

iii

Postmodernist criticism has recently burgeoned in three major new directions, besides the older approaches such as Marxism, Freudianism, and others that have long been well established in our institutional literary life: deconstructionism, the "new historicism," and feminism. Each of these new schools has had important literary-sociological effects that are linked to its philosophical aims. First, Jacques Derrida set off an enormous outpouring of critical studies with his linguistic insights; he and his followers engendered a powerful critical tide that appears to have begun to ebb somewhat, at least in the United States.[10] A legacy of the school appears to be the radical skepticism about language and value that has become part of the postmodernist critical vocabulary, as "free play," and "textuality," and the like.[11]

As the theorist John M. Ellis has observed, using the Saussurian terminology of "signs,"

> The idea that signs play infinitely and indiscriminately against each other is one that is . . . an impossible one to justify. To be recognizable as *anything*, a sign must have a distinctive shape and function that recognizably sets it apart from other signs. To postulate a sign that simply played indefinitely and infinitely against other signs is to imagine one with no distinct character at all, i.e., one not recognizable as having any shape or function of its own. That produces not more and richer meaning, as advocates of this position like to think, but no meaning at all. A sign not recognizable as anything in particular signifies nothing whatsoever. *Vagueness* in signs introduces diminution, not augmentation, of meaning. Complete vagueness, complete indefiniteness of signification is the point at which zero signification is reached.

But not only is this argument erroneous in itself; it is also used by its advocates in the mistaken belief that it is needed to support a particular kind of step in criticism for which it is, in fact, quite unnecessary. It is very commonly used as general theoretical support for a particular critic's finding subtleties and added meaning that had not previously been visible to critics who concentrated too much on the obvious surface meanings of words. But situations such as this do not call for a new theory of signification; all that is needed is to show that previous criticism has been superficial and incomplete in its account of what the text signifies and to offer a more inclusive and complex view of its meaning. Anyone who thinks that this kind of critical move requires a view of signification as infinite and indeterminate is only misdescribing what he has just done: he has not shown infinite meaning but instead additional, *specifically stated* meaning that had been ignored in an inadequate account of the text. The critic has shown something *particular*; he deludes himself if he thinks he has shown something indeterminate and indiscriminate. This is as true of Derrida as anyone else who, when he begins to talk about a text, makes particular assertions and takes specific positions on them; indeed, it could not be otherwise.[12]

How does this free play work in practice? By beginning from the genuinely protean nature of language itself, the postmodernist critic can take any particular example of language in a literary work and reveal its hidden self-contradictions and moments of ambiguity. In this way, the critic asserts a kind of control over the work of art, a control that perhaps substitutes in some fashion for the value that the postmodernist is unwilling to claim.

I believe, however, that a simpler response to this real complexity of language and words is available. As Ellis implies, understanding the limits of language and the concomitant difficulties of communication is an important cautionary insight with which to begin any philosophical study. But we must take care not to begin the quest for meaning and secure philosophical ground too heavily armed for the dangers that lie ahead. Certainly, language can be crushed under the weight of its own limitations. It *is* an inadequate map or grid placed on experience—experience that it of course helps to structure. It *does* push us toward one sort of bias or another, depending on our assumptions and preconceptions. These are conditions, however, that call for tact and care in questioning our beliefs, not radical skepticism. As the philosopher Ludwig Wittgenstein has noted, "From [a thing's] *seeming* to me—or to everyone—to be so, it doesn't follow that it *is* so. What we can ask is whether it can make sense to doubt it."[13] In arguing that most attempts at definition are really better understood as instructions about how to behave, Wittgenstein asks us to confront attempts to "unmask" the precariousness of language with the tactful assertion that there are points when it simply no longer makes sense to doubt. In language, "A meaning of a word is a kind of employment of it"; as such *the very goal itself of fixing meaning—or determining that it is unfixable—is a mistaken goal.* He says that "the difficulty is to realize the groundlessness of our believing," while at the same time recognizing the importance of continuing to believe. "If my name is *not* L. W., how can I rely on what is meant by 'true' and 'false'?"[14]

We critics, in short, must seek to explore and to understand the meaningful limits of language with sensitivity and discretion even as we rigorously examine our own preconceptions. Because the task of decoding meaningful (written) communication may be limited and imperfect does not mean that it cannot usefully be done.

Proponents of both new historicism and feminism have at times begun from a radically skeptical philosophical orientation and at times have rejected that slippery ground.[15] Just as deconstructionism in effect expanded the canon enormously with its relativistic concept of the intertextuality of all written works, however, both of the other two schools have widened not only the canon but also what constitutes literary evidence, bringing much new cultural and social research to bear on literary studies as well as the readership of it.[16]

Our search for a flexible, useful theory of criticism by which to approach the works of Dickens will attempt to escape both the Scylla of the radical instability of language and the Charybdis of too narrowly restricting our task. Again, I believe that the fundamental role of criticism is to enliven and illumine the reading experience. But we do not play tennis without a net—or rackets and balls. All critics seek—and postmodernists are no exception—to correct what they see as distortions in previous attitudes toward the issues of text and canon, author and reader, context and meaning.

Further, all reading is directed by specific configurations of assumptions and interests; all interpretation is provisional and limited. I turn to Dickens with the knowledge that my reading, like all others, must stand or fall on its persuasiveness for other readers. To claim otherwise would be epistemologically naïve. Thus, what follows lays out my own Dickensian program and points out some of the pitfalls that can trap readers of his complex, multifarious novels.

iv

Dickensian critics need a well-grounded methodology and set of presuppositions that can systematically analyze Dickens's multifarious universe. The methodology must be flexible: Dickens's world teems with self-contradictions. It must also be consistent, else we will merely yield to eclecticism—an a priori admission of philosophical failure. But ever since G. K.

Chesterton's delightful work on Dickens, critics have too often based their literary judgments solely on biographical ones.[17] The Dickensian feels obliged to come to terms with the blacking warehouse episode in Dickens's youth, the difficult marriage in his middle age, and the affair with Ellen Ternan in his later years in order to do justice to the fiction.[18] But such *biographical* details, it must be remembered, are necessary but not sufficient to explaining the *artist*. How many Victorians worked in blacking factories? How many had difficult marriages, how many affairs? Dickens is not remarkable because he had these experiences but because of his reactions to them. We must take care not to let Dickens the man obscure his literary works; mining the works for biography and the biography for the works is an all too appealing but finally vicious circle. Indeed, the remarkable character of the man makes this trap an easy one into which to fall.

Another danger, and one to which all works of art are vulnerable, is the urge to measure Dickens's novels by some insufficiently acknowledged standard and then cut the works to fit the measurements. The novels are distorted to fill requirements established by a twentieth-century artist or philosopher—transforming Dickens into James, for example, or making him conform to Georges Bataille.[19] Finally, the understandable desire to produce a coherent picture of the entire messy Dickensian universe pushes some to mistake the part for the whole, inflating a partial truth until it resembles an exhaustive treatment. As a result, one reads heroic but misguided efforts such as *The Dickens World, Charles Dickens: The World of His Novels*, and *The World of Charles Dickens*; or one reads of the "resurrectionist," the "dreamer's stance," the "myth," the "popular entertainment," and the "theatre" of Dickens.[20] Often a study that begins as a useful corrective to the current state of Dickensian criticism overemphasizes a new aspect of Dickens's work, necessitating yet another corrective.[21] Dickens's oeuvre remains too many-sided to be (adequately) reduced to one, even large and powerful, insight.

Studying these near misses raises a crucial theoretical issue. What is relevant to the study of literature? What is extraliterary? Certainly, of course, research on Dickens's life has an important role to play in the development of an adequate criticism of his art. But the perils of overemphasizing the biography are clear.[22] We need to find another starting point.

If we concentrate instead on the questions raised by a particular "situated" reader's direct experience of the text, we will discover a more useful beginning orientation.[23] Such a position will lead inevitably to questions about Dickens's nineteenth-century milieu and his own life, but only after one has first studied the interaction of twentieth-century readers with all their particular preconceptions and the nineteenth-century text. This critical study would seek to remain as long as possible in the realm of the verb, not of the noun, attempting a dynamic study of the fusing of a modern reader's conjugating of the text with the text as *it* is situated culturally. Thus we will not lose track of what it means to read a Dickensian novel in a fascination with reconstructions of the historical personage who produced them. Research on both the biography and the period will be guided by questions that arise in reading rather than the reverse.

Such a rapid glance at Dickensian criticism and its typical problems leads one to question the very undertaking, the project of interpreting so large an oeuvre by so complex an author. One wonders if there is any point in attempting to reduce the experience of reading fifteen novels and innumerable shorter works to one book-length piece. My argument at once suggests that the Dickensian universe is ultimately irreducible. I believe that we must begin the study of Dickens, or indeed any writer, with our attention fixed firmly on a particular experience of reading—or rereading—the author's works. I do not seek to be too wise before I begin, determined to find one single key to this multifarious whole. Reoriented in such a manner, the goal of criticism becomes the illumination of the dynamics of that textual experience, *not* the discovery of some hitherto unguessed, usually startling, central truth about Dickens the novelist.[24] In short, the verb, not the noun. Beginning with reading the text further relieves me of the burden of necessarily finding some grand synthesis of the whole. Mine is a more limited, humbler task. I begin my research prepared to sacrifice the reductive coherence of many studies of Dickens that search for confirmation of some a priori, all-encompassing plan. At the same time, the present method will free me to recognize the patterns that emerge in the reading of an individual novel and in the comparison of that novel to others written by the same author. If Dickens's fifteen novels and other works create a group capable of characterization by its family resemblances and differences, then a method that focuses on illuminating the textual dynamics of that novelistic family should be able to provide an adequate model of the Dickensian universe.[25]

It seems to me that the only a priori judgment one can make about the Dickensian universe is that it represents a pluralistic *collection*, not a unified, internally consistent *system*, of artworks. Dickens's novels constitute a group of highly controlled yet dynamic subsets of language. It is vital to stress the dynamism of the novels, lest one fall into the trap of reifying one's terms even before beginning to read. The nature of our linguistic heritage makes it almost impossible to argue at length without treating novelistic processes as products. Thus "reading" almost inevitably becomes "a reading" in the event of its formulation. If we simply acknowledge at this point, however, that we discuss "novels," knowing that in fact we mean what happens when one particular person sits down *to read*, then we may preserve our theoretical integrity. Texts only come to life in their re-creations by readers; when we critics discuss literature, we base our arguments on our memories of a dynamic process, reading.

The dynamic nature of literature underscores its status as a special kind of language, a unique form of communication that nonetheless makes up part of the larger set. One plays a literary game, or a variety of literary games, in reading. These games have rules governing their conduct, just as the parent set of language does. Indeed, I can find no logical reason to separate the subset of literature from language as a whole. Just as Kant was wrong to segregate art, calling it aesthetic where other objects, man-made and natural, were useful, so too does one err in segregating literature from language. Literature attempts to persuade others of some truth, whether debased or noble, just as language does. Both form part of that infinitely various human game called communication. In playing that game, one tries to convince those who will listen of the worth of what one has to say. The language that works the best survives the longest. The tendency among some literary critical circles to separate literature from language, then, commits the Kantian error once again with less justification.[26]

If language is persuasion, literature must then be a particular kind of persuasion. John M. Ellis offers a useful first attempt at definition. "Literary texts are defined as those that are used by society in such a way that the text is not taken as specifically relevant to the immediate context of its origin."[27] I would modify Ellis's definition by noting that rather than not being "specifically relevant" to its origin, literature both refers to its original context and goes beyond it. When one reads, one tends to apply the particular story one experiences to one's larger knowledge of human nature, or love, or the like. Readers allegorize what they read; literature speaks at once to the era of its creation and to one's own, or it falls silent. For all readers, literature has both a literal level and a level of application, a "symbolic" level. I do not mean to suggest that one first reads and then interprets.[28] Rather, every act of reading is an act of interpretation.[29] In other words, each interpretation begins with one particular reader reading. To break the process down into two discrete steps is misleading, because reading is a process of simultaneously interpreting the story in terms of what one has already experienced and reflecting on the changes that reading brings about in one's psyche, by applying what one learns to one's knowledge of life. The circle does not become vicious unless the critic fails to follow both of the tasks that hermeneutics sets. When we enter the circle, we commit ourselves to the search both for particulars that support our general presuppositions and for contrary evidence that modifies our theories.[30]

In Dickens's case, the nineteenth-century origin of the text complicates the job of interpretation. Some critics would argue that readers should attempt to determine as best they can what authors intended, learning as much as possible about writers, their use of language, and the time in which they wrote.[31] Under this approach, critics subordinate their own predilections to the text's, to the extent that the text reflects their reconstructed author. The difficulties inherent in such an approach are clear, however, in light of Dickensian critics who erect psychological statues of Dickens the man, obscuring the works they should be studying. Critics who try to achieve a complete understanding of the author's intentions work toward a spurious goal of objectivity. Objectivity eludes the grasp of literary critics; they mistake their role if they seek it. Criticism rather seeks to convince the largest audience it can of the persuasiveness of its views.

An ultimately more useful aim for critics is to achieve a fusion of their own perspective with their understanding of the period.[32] When we read a nineteenth-century work, its historical aspects cannot fail to strike us. Quite simply, a nineteenth-century work reveals its origins on every page. The text uses language differently than twentieth-century speakers do, and the concerns of the characters do not match twentieth-century concerns. Nonetheless, enough of the text does speak to modern interests to enable us to understand some part of it, or we would not continue to read the novel, play, or poem. When we read with full recognition of our status as twentieth-century readers of a nineteenth-century novel, we make possible the greatest apprehension of the range of meanings available to historically situated readers. We both recognize the inevitable and make it a strength in order to exploit both the strengths and weaknesses of our special historical vantage point. When Dickens writes about the effects of the accumulated waste of civilization in *Our Mutual Friend*, for example, twentieth-century readers may engage Dickens's satire with a more profound knowledge of many of the consequences of developments that Dickens noted in their early stages. Or when the narrator of *Our Mutual Friend* attempts to enter into the mind of a murderer, Bradley Headstone, latter-day readers may estimate more fully the narrator's successes and failures, benefiting from a century of further psychological study, both Freudian and neo-Freudian in the largest sense.

I pause here to acknowledge the extent that modern critics of psychology are all neo-Freudian, to a greater or lesser degree. Even those who desire to do so cannot completely escape the legacy that Freud created for us, drawing on much thinking (by Nietzsche, Schopenhauer, and other philosophers) that was current in the nineteenth century. Further, though, modern critics inevitably are *neo*-Freudians when we perform psychological analyses of character in the sense that we attempt to improve on a theory still at times useful for the epistemological insights it offers, yet often flawed in its particular psychological constructions. Moreover, Freud himself stands midway between Dickens's Victorian universe and our own modern era.[33] Thus this psychological theory in itself begins the process of fusion of perspectives that we must accomplish as literary critics. Freudian psychology speaks both to the issues of the nineteenth century and the twentieth. It gives us a terminology by which we may begin to analyze the characters a Victorian novelist has created without having to make a futile effort to abandon the twentieth century. In a sense, then, the first step toward a fusion has already been accomplished for us: We have a linguistic bridge into the past.

Some cautionary notes about this powerful analytical tool are in order, however. Freudian theory above all else seeks to strip away the superficial meanings to which one gives credence in everyday life.[34] Freud looks for a latent meaning beneath the surface one, for deeper psychological motivations for apparently trivial acts. He hopes, in other words, to unmask the psyche of his patients, to show them the inner workings of their soul. The latent meaning that is exposed will consist of patients' originally unconscious desires, fears, and most important, memories. For Freud, the engine that drives neurotics down their one-way track is their set of traumatic memories. Once those memories become conscious, available to the victims, they may be able to understand and finally control their irrational wishes and fears. Thus one of the most vital tasks of Freudian analysts consists of an *archaeological* exploration of the past of their patients.[35] A similar task falls to literary critics. They too hunt for the *arche*, the hidden engine that drives a novel's characters and gives structure to its prose. Indeed, more specifically, one's understanding of a particular novel often begins with its characters, and to comprehend their psyches one delves into their pasts as represented in the fiction.

But the danger that awaits this exercise in unmasking, in laying bare hidden secrets, comes from the very flexibility and adaptability of the (Freudian) model. Because Freud's theory represents so powerful a tool for digging beneath surface meanings to expose to the air the buried ones, the psychologist risks succumbing to the temptation to explain too much, to reduce an entire world of meaning to a few complexes. The same temptation awaits the literary critic. In fact, many a Freudian literary critic has been seduced by the allure of easy explanation in reading Dickens.[36] One must not forget, as one strips away layer after layer of meaning, searching for the buried *arche* that gives energy to the rest, that one's goal as critic remains re-creation of the dynamic, particular experience of reading the text—limited and partial though the final result will inevitably be.

To compensate for the reductive tendencies of this sort of theory, I construct a dialectic that takes me back to the surface after so much work below. If I pursue an archaeology into a reading experience of nineteenth-century fiction, then, I must also re-create a teleology. My second goal must be the delineation of the *telos* of the Dickensian novel. As one strips away the levels of meaning that animate the symbolism of a culture, one must remember that the people who possess that culture live from day to day by those very levels of meaning. In taking possession of a novel, we must take care to temper the implicit arrogance of the archaeological model with the humility of a celebration of that novel and its symbolism in an unviolated state. The surface meanings are finally no less important than the latent ones in my own willed and limited re-creation of the experience of reading a Dickensian text.

As Paul Ricoeur argues in *Freud and Philosophy*, the two dialectical movements do not represent unrelated activities. Our dialectic remains flexible yet internally consistent. Just as Freud himself moved from archaeological analysis to teleological musings in his life's work, so too particular moments in Freudian theory suggest teleological direction even as they perform archaeological exploration. The concept of sublimation, for example, shows that the *arche* of the soul, the unconscious, must go beyond itself to satisfy its needs. The id, in other words, seeks transcendence. From such unconscious yearnings comes the symbolism humankind establishes to express the frustrations inherent in this earthly state of infinite longing and finite ability to satisfy that longing.[37] The soul demands constant excess, forever going beyond itself to express and to attempt to satisfy its needs. Language, after all, evolves as the expression of those needs. Indeed, Freudian language, by making new use of ancient terminology such as the Oedipal myth, has an implicit archaeological and teleological dialectic of its own. Finally, the format of traditional Freudian psychotherapy has a teleological issue even as it explores the *arche* of the patient. The goal of therapy takes the patient from bondage to his wishes and fears in ignorance to the freedom of rational control in full self-knowledge. The dialectic I am developing similarly derives from the fusion of the nineteenth- and twentieth-century perspectives and my humility in the face of the transient nature of all culture. The language of symbol and the language of dreams must unite in our literary pursuit of one reader's dynamic reconstruction of reading a Dickensian novel.

I have chosen as examples *The Old Curiosity Shop, David Copperfield, Little Dorrit*, and *Great Expectations*. These four novels span Dickens's literary career and fairly represent the major phases of his development as a novelist; thus these works will amply demonstrate the flexibility of my methodology. Specifically, *The Old Curiosity Shop* typifies Dickens's early work in its extremes of character and situation and challenges modern readers to exercise their historical understanding in engaging the (by our standards) sentimental text. *David Copperfield* and *Great Expectations* form a natural diptych that contrasts Dickens's work in middle and late career,

and yet provides a continuity of form in the first-person narrative. Finally, *Little Dorrit* typifies the period of the social novel, the 1850s, the period that for many represents Dickens at the height of his powers.[38] I strive
to read *Little Dorrit* without succumbing to the temptation to make the
work the *sine qua non* of some grand unifying vision of "The Dickens
World"; I seek to put the novel, in other words, in a sensible perspective,
one that suggests the entire Dickensian career in all its multifariousness.

I create a model of that multifarious Dickensian universe by following
primarily three aspects of the reading experience through the four novels.
Study of the relationship between reader and narrator, especially in its moral
dimensions, will help us understand nineteenth-century perspectives. A
narrative dialectic between the power of the imagination and the restraint
of authority or discipline provides the motivation, in varying degrees, for
many of the personal odysseys that the reader encounters in the texts. Finally, our archaeological pursuit of the buried secrets in the characters' memories combines with our teleological exploration of the symbolic life of the
narrative to produce the dialectic that structures our reading.

The narrator of *The Old Curiosity Shop* says of Little Nell that "she
seemed to exist in a kind of allegory."[39] The problem for twentieth-century readers has been in comprehending clearly the consistent yet broadly
drawn nature of that allegorical presence. Wherever Nell wanders on her
Victorian pilgrimage, she excites in those she meets a need to provide the
homeless child with a home. She domesticates the strangers whom she
encounters on her way; they immediately wish to worship at her homely
shrine. Quilp, on the other hand, personifies the seamy side of the world
of work. The demonic imp revels in crooked business deals and petty
schemes, celebrating his wicked energies with an enthusiasm at times astonishing. The two together represent opposites at either end of a continuous
chain of desire; both ultimately embrace death because life for them has
become intolerable. As obviously dissimilar as they are in many ways,
both Nell and Quilp are alike in willing their own deaths when they find
that their desires cannot be fulfilled.

The narrator of *David Copperfield* discusses his self-appointed task in
a deceptively simple passage that conceals as much of his attitude as it
reveals: "In fulfillment of the compact I have made with myself, to reflect
my mind on this paper, I again examine it, closely, and bring its secrets to
life."[40] The narrator's comment suggests that he attempts a self-analysis.
He performs his own archaeological digging, endeavoring to uncover the
buried mysteries of his own soul. At the same time, however, he constructs
a teleology out of his self-analysis. As he ponders the passages in his life,
he develops his own individual mythology by selecting those events that
matter most to him. As readers beginning to know David more fully, we

must at once resist his efforts to charm us into easy acceptance of his version of events and yet embrace his story in order to master it as a whole. David fights a dialectical battle with himself; he pits David the dreamer against David the self-disciplined worker. As readers, we must perform a dialectical investigation of our own before we take sides in the struggle between restraint and the license of dreams.

Little Dorrit gives the reader a picture of Victorian England as a chaos of solipsistic prisons, a picture that pushes the reader to attempt to discover some means of escape. Arthur Clennam leaves one prison, quarantine in Marseilles, to return to England and the imprisonment of his youth. Arthur's drear childhood lent urgency to self-assertion in his own private world of fancy as a boy; Arthur returns to the scene of his childhood and his mother's domination in part to rediscover the need to assert himself in his lonely bachelorhood. The dialectical struggle between "fancy" and an imprisoning authority in *Little Dorrit* contains some surprising ambiguities; fancy plays most freely amid restraint and often seems to require authority to give it impetus. The idea of escape from the prisons in the novel becomes for the reader a complex and disturbing one; the character who succeeds in at least temporary escape may find that fancy after all imprisons itself, that no permanent escape can be possible. Finally, the novel leaves the reader perplexed about any teleological issue; the *telos* that the text delineates for its readers exists only in opposition to the world at hand. *Little Dorrit* does not share with us a compelling vision of the world to come even as the novel attempts to comfort its readers with an uncertain promise of otherworldly escape.

Pip's visions constitute the heart of the experience of reading *Great Expectations*. From the start, the novel is remarkable for what it tells and what it does not tell. *Great Expectations* teems with secrets. No narrator retains total control over his tale, however; Pip may unwittingly disclose truths about himself that he wishes to keep hidden. Moreover, Pip may reveal unconsciously to the reader what he does not know consciously about himself. Pip does exactly that, indeed, with the language of hands in the novel. What a character says with his hands can contradict his spoken words, revealing his unspoken designs. With their hands, the characters in *Great Expectations* signal their ability or lack thereof to manipulate the other characters in the novel. The language of hands in the book is the language of control. The dialectical alternation between revelation and concealment places heavy demands on the reader to make his own archaeological connections where the narrator remains silent. The teleological bent of *Great Expectations*, toward self-knowledge on the part of the narrator, can be the reader's too; reading *Great Expectations* returns the willing reader to that dark place in his or her fancy where the authority of the inner voice can only just keep the remembered demons of childhood at bay.

These four novels direct their readers to make moral decisions about characters and events, the ends of which readers largely know even as they pick the texts up for the first time to begin their journey. Nowhere in the Dickensian universe does fancy revel without limitations; the struggles it undergoes against the restrictions of authority, indeed, give life to its efforts at creation. In the first of the four works I discuss here, readers must confront the inescapable pathos of Little Nell's doomed effort to impose her fancy on an inflexible nineteenth-century England, an effort mimicked both by other characters in the Dickensian universe and perhaps even by readers themselves in worlds of their own.

2

The Angel and the Imp

Divine Kalypso,
the mistress of the isle, was now at home.
Upon her hearthstone a great fire blazing
scented the farthest shores with cedar smoke
and smoke of thyme, and singing high and low
in her sweet voice, before her loom a-weaving,
she passed her golden shuttle to and fro.
A deep wood grew outside, with summer leaves
of alder and black poplar, pungent cypress.
Ornate birds here rested their stretched wings—
horned owls, falcons, cormorants—long-tongued
beachcombing birds, and followers of the sea.
Around the smoothwalled cave a crooking vine
held purple clusters under ply of green;
and four springs, bubbling up near one another
shallow and clear, took channels here and there
through beds of violets and tender parsley.
Homer, *Odyssey* 5.55–71

Oscar Wilde remarked that one would need a heart of stone not to laugh at the death of Little Nell, and his comment still haunts modern critics of *The Old Curiosity Shop*. The novel remains important to Dickensian scholars because it typifies Dickens's early career with its sharp sentimentality and challenges the modern reader in that its very sentimentality, in large part, made it the most popular of the early novels.[1] The question becomes, in this light, how can we modern critics read *The Old Curiosity Shop* in a way that does justice to our prior sensibilities as well as to those that arise from our reading, without ignoring large parts of the novel? We must be prepared for the answer that we can no longer read *The Old Curiosity Shop* for any pleasure or instruction, save of an antiquarian sort alone.

But a way of reading the novel that meets these strictures does, I think,

Little Nell and her Grandfather
The Old Curiosity Shop

exist. If we focus on a particular modern reader's concrete experience of grappling with a text that at certain moments speaks across the years to our present-day concerns and at other moments remains lost to us in the past, we may consider *The Old Curiosity Shop* with interest at least, if not perhaps finally with love.[2] We may also discover that passages in the novel usually thought to have meaning only for the original audience can in fact instruct and delight both the Victorian and the modern reader.

Focusing on the historicity of a nineteenth-century work does not make the "Victorian reading" the only correct one. It is not prescriptive. Rather, it is invitational. An investigation of *The Old Curiosity Shop* that stresses modern attempts to read an early Victorian novel can clearly delineate those aspects of the text that will interest both the twentieth-century reader and the Victorian. Our goal is a fusion of the two perspectives, not a rejection of either.[3] Thus we will achieve a position from which we may bring the text most fully to life, because *unself-consciously* parochial modern attitudes will not impede our analysis of parochial Victorian attitudes when they arise in the work. Finally, the present approach will be able to confront directly the sentimental parts of the novel that recent critics have shied away from and to describe more precisely what troubles the modern reader about this "most difficult [of] fictions."[4]

i

The Old Curiosity Shop begins with an old man's solicitude for a young girl. The beginnings of fictions merit our special attention because they establish the expectations that readers have for the rest of the work. In this manner, they shape our subsequent experience of the text. Here, Master Humphrey finds himself instantly attracted to the child who seems to arise from his dreams, a fairy child, a child of the night and its attendant shadows. When Little Nell asks him to escort her home, the old man's intense, paternal response comes immediately:

> I cannot describe how much I was impressed by this appeal, and the energy with which it was made, which brought a tear into the child's clear eye, and made her slight figure tremble as she looked up into my face.
> "Come," said I, "I'll take you there."
> She put her hand in mine, as confidingly as if she had known me from her cradle, and we trudged away together: the little creature accommodating her pace to mine, and rather seeming to lead and take care of me than I to be protecting her. I observed that every now and then she stole a curious look at my face as if to make quite sure that I was not deceiving her, and

that these glances (very sharp and keen they were too) seemed to increase her confidence at every repetition.[5]

Little Nell never becomes any more worldly than at this moment when we first meet her in the street. The narrator never applies the words "sharp" and "keen" to her again. In fact, Nell grows more and more ethereal and otherworldly. Similarly, the old men in the novel become, if anything, even more solicitous than Master Humphrey. Little Nell's ability to excite a desire in male characters to protect her only increases the deeper into the novel the reader goes.

And what a large number of old men one finds in *The Old Curiosity Shop*. Mr. Garland, the Notary, the Sexton, Dave, the Sexton's friend, the Curate, the Bachelor, the Schoolmaster, the Lodger, even Abel Garland, who is old in everything except years, and of course Nell's grandfather himself. We find few middle-aged male characters and even fewer younger ones, but the novel teems with old men. Whenever Nell pauses in her wanderings long enough to become known among the townspeople, the narrator surrounds her with solicitous elderly gentlemen. The reader wonders why; what is the author up to? What does Nell represent that she should provoke such a response? Master Humphrey's initial reaction to Nell will give us some hints.

Little Nell interests Master Humphrey enormously. He describes her as full of "energy" and suggests that she leads him along, rather than the reverse. We may conclude, therefore, that at a simple level the girl's youthful freshness and strength attract an old man whose life energies approach their ebb. Master Humphrey responds to more than the mere opposition of youth and age, however.

Images of enclosure, captivity, and burden fill the first chapter of *The Old Curiosity Shop*. The "sick man" in "Saint Martin's Court" is "obliged, despite himself (as though it were a task he must perform) to detect the child's step from the man's, the slipshod beggar from the booted exquisite, the lounging from the busy, the dull heel of the sauntering outcast from the quick tread of an expectant pleasure seeker"(P. 1). His illness traps him, forcing him to endure the intrusions of an unmannerly world. The bridges over which Master Humphrey passes on his walks remind him of suicides prompted by heavy "loads" (P. 2) of a physical sort that correspond to the psychic burden the observer himself carries. Nell becomes the old man's burden, ensnaring him by arousing in him a strong desire to protect her. She too carries a burden, a secret that she must protect. Finally, as we watch the two wanderers arrive at the shop, we become aware that it represents, at least in Master Humphrey's mind, an exotic enclosure, even a trap, in which the old man has caught his granddaughter. Master Humphrey slowly realizes that the old man in some ways depends on Little Nell as much as she does on him, or perhaps even more.

Thus, not only Nell's youth works to produce the extraordinary sense of claustrophobia that Master Humphrey conjures up in the first chapter. Nell's seeming helplessness, her ostentatious innocence, her virginal femininity—these traits further explain the intense paternal need that Nell awakens in the desiccated old men whom she meets.

But the narrator attempts to do more in the first chapter than impress the reader with Nell's extraordinary qualities. A passage near the end of the chapter offers some clues to his aims:

> We are so much in the habit of allowing impressions to be made upon us by external objects . . . , that I am not sure I should have been so thoroughly possessed by this one subject, but for the heaps of fantastic things I had seen huddled together in the curiosity-dealer's warehouse. These, crowding on my mind, in connection with the child, and gathering around her, as it were, brought her condition palpably before me. I had her image, without any effort of imagination, surrounded and beset by everything that was foreign to its nature, and farthest removed from the sympathies of her sex and age. If these helps to my fancy had all been wanting, and I had been forced to imagine her in a common chamber, with nothing unusual or uncouth in its appearance, it is very probable that I should have been less impressed with her strange and solitary state. *As it was, she seemed to exist in a kind of allegory*; and, having these shapes about her, claimed my interest so strongly, that . . . I could not dismiss her from my recollections, do what I would. (P. 13, emphasis added)

The narrator creates, through Master Humphrey's musings, the grounds on which the "kind of allegory" that *The Old Curiosity Shop* represents can work in the reader's experience of the text. If the reader can entertain the important symbolic relationships, reading *The Old Curiosity Shop* will have an allegorical quality. The problem for readers after Dickens's death has been understanding clearly the consistent yet broadly drawn nature of the allegory.

The first clue comes from Master Humphrey's insistence on the importance of the "heaps of fantastic things" that surround Nell and help his fancy transmute his sensations from the humdrum into the unusual. The child's homely manners seem to make the shop her own, not the old man's. As a result, the things in her bizarre abode cluster about *her*; she domesticates them. Nell thus evokes, despite the unpromising milieu, domesticity. Wherever she goes on her Victorian pilgrimage, Little Nell carries an overpowering aura of the homeless child in need of a Home. How can the reader respond to such a character?

Not as someone fully three-dimensional. Master Humphrey treats Nell as an allegorical figure for the first few chapters, after which he drops out

of the narrative. At the end of chapter 1, Master Humphrey places Nell
amid the strange objects of the shop in a way that makes her just another
object, if the most extraordinary one in the shop. He manipulates her "image"
in his mind to satisfy his daydream. In other words, he reduces Nell's nascent
humanity to a symbol. For him, as well as for virtually all the other characters she meets, she powerfully evokes the need for a Home. For the characters in *The Old Curiosity Shop* as well as for its Victorian readers, Nell
embodies the "Angel without a House" like no other literary creation.[6]

Thus modern readers who find themselves impatient with what they see
as Nell's impossible goodness or her insufferable humility do so because
they have difficulty responding to the clues the novel provides for its allegorical reading. The Victorian had less trouble. Accustomed to ponder-
ing Thomas Carlyle on "Herr Teufelsdrockh" and "Blumine," the Victorian
would more easily think of Little Nell as a static symbol whenever she
appears.[7] Victorian painters, too, taught their middle-class audiences to
find symbolic virtues and vices for the realistic figures in their works.
George Cruikshank's series on the dangers of *The Bottle* is perhaps the
most famous example among many similar drawings.[8]

Modern readers are accustomed, however, to parables when they read
allegory at all. *Animal Farm, The Lord of the Flies*—these allegories work
as wholes, every literal moment charged with a specific symbolic meaning. Nonetheless, many readers, when they pick up a novel, allegorize
what they read in a general sense. They find the book more or less pleas-
ing, indeed, depending on what it tells them about the human condition, or
the nature of love, or the like. Readers apply the immediate situation in
the story to themselves and to what they know of the world in order to
derive personal meaning from the fiction. As modern readers of *The Old
Curiosity Shop*, then, we may use our general understanding of the allegorical aspect of reading to comprehend the specific form that it takes in
this early Victorian novel. In this way, we moderns may engage this nineteenth-century, bourgeois *Pilgrim's Progress*. Unable to allegorize precisely as the Victorians did, we do not submit here to a "Victorian
reading." Rather we fuse our modern awareness of the process of reading
with a particular nineteenth-century example. We may understand Nell's
evocation of the home virtues without necessarily embracing such Victorian values. It remains for us to discuss how Nell's allegorical presence
affects the rest of the narrative and how the other characters, but most
notably Quilp, function within the allegory.

When Nell's grandfather falls ill, the evil Quilp causes the old man unrea-
sonably to suspect Kit Nubbles of having a hand in his master's downfall.
Kit then makes a desperate effort to restore himself to Nell's good graces:

"It's not that I may be taken back," said the boy, "that I ask the favour of
you. It isn't for the sake of food and wages that I've been waiting about, so
long, in hopes to see you. Don't think that I'd come in a time of trouble to
talk of such things as them."

The child [Nell] looked gratefully and kindly at him, but waited that he
might speak again.

"No, it's not that," said Kit hesitating, "it's something very different from
that . . . This home is gone from you and him. Mother and I have got a poor
one, but that's better than this with all these people here; and why not come
there, till he's had time to look about, and find a better!" (Pp. 88–89)

Kit's rather formal conversation and Nell's response suggest two important ways that this apparently trivial moment contributes to the development of the narrative as a whole. First, Kit joins with Master Humphrey
and Nell's grandfather and a host of other characters in the novel who
respond almost instinctively to Nell's temporary homelessness by attempting to create a substitute home for her. The characters wish to construct
about her a domestic altar at which she may become a permanent Presence. Consequently, they find themselves frustrated by Nell's tendency to
uproot herself and her grandfather and vanish, as if her home were not on
this earth. After Kit's failed attempt, the reader witnesses Codlin and
Short's efforts to attach themselves to Nell. Nell senses, however, that the
two traveling artists act out of mercenary rather than pious motives. With
the virgin's instinctive knack for survival, she convinces her terrified grandfather to abandon the two scoundrels. After a brief domestic idyll with the
poor Schoolmaster, Nell finds another temporary home with Mrs. Jarley,
who also immediately desires to provide for her security. Nell's final earthly haven, the quiet country town, quickly envelops her in a homely embrace,
as if ineffectually trying to persuade her to remain on earth, at Home.

Such a brief recitation of the allegorical structure of the novel shows
that, in the largest sense, Nell's symbolic journey involves successive
attempts to create a home worthy of her and successive disruptions of those
havens. The final disruption, Nell's last illness, resolves the question of
Nell's fitness for the world by sending her to an eternal home. Thus the
symbolic level of the story prepares its readers for Nell's death by creating a teleology that leads inexorably to her last peregrination.

Kit's efforts to create a little home for Nell, with her as a captive goddess fit only for worship, prepares us further for the death of the heroine.
Nell's response to Kit's entreaties may perhaps surprise us. In a wordy
novel, in an era of wordy novels, Nell says nothing. Indeed, it is characteristic of Nell to say nothing except when need compels her. Little Nell
does not prattle, unlike Kit, and unlike most of the other children in the
novel. Typical examples are the Schoolmaster's favorite pupil and Nell's

friend, who has a "cruel dream" (P. 530) in the village at journey's end. Such reticence in Nell must strike us as extraordinary for a Dickensian child, especially one who attracts as much emotional and symbolic attention as Nell does. What can Nell's strange silences mean?

To begin with, Nell usually says nothing because she does not need to say anything. Most people, let alone children, would rush to fill the awkward silences with words. Little Nell possesses the security to let the silences remain. Nell's own perfect innocence leads her to attribute a similar innocence to most of the other characters. It takes strong evidence to the contrary, such as the sort she receives from Quilp or Codlin and Short, to force her to believe somebody capable of evil. In a world full of innocents, all would employ words for the same purpose that Nell does: simple communication. When characters pursue nefarious schemes, however, they must repair the thin places in the fabric of their deceptions with knots of words. Even the other children, while hardly villains, are not as simple as Nell. She remains complete, and silent, in her innocence. Like Carlyle's William the Silent in *Sartor Resartus*, for Nell, "Speech is of Time, Silence is of Eternity" (bk.3, chap. 3). Further, her reticence has a teleological aspect that suggests her ultimate role in the novel. Her conversational silence prefigures the more profound silence of death. Her deliberate withdrawal from worldly communication mirrors her later, equally deliberate withdrawal from the world itself. The talkativeness of the other children in the novel demonstrates their will to live. Nell does not love the world and its *words* too much, lest she should become ensnared in them.

When Nell and her grandfather first withdraw from London, the move may well strike us as one of the few efforts that Nell makes to preserve her life. She wants to escape, one thinks, the London of Quilp and creditors—the apparent causes of her grandfather's downfall. Nell dreams of a peaceful existence in a country town where she and her grandfather may tend their little cottage and garden and so find rest at last from the turmoil of London. The prose with which the narrator describes their exit, however, echoes with more disturbing implications:

> This was a wide, wide track—for the humble followers of the camp of wealth pitch their tents round about it for many a mile—but its character was still the same. Damp rotten houses, many to let, many yet building, many half-built and mouldering away—lodgings, where it would be hard to tell which needed pity most, those who let or those who came to take—children, scantily fed and clothed . . . and sprawling in the dust—scolding mothers, stamping their slipshod feet with noisy threats upon the pavement—shabby fathers, hurrying . . . to the occupation which brought them "daily bread" and little more—mangling-women, washerwomen, cobblers, tailors, chandlers, driving their trades in parlours and kitchens and back rooms and garretts, . . .

brickfields . . . , mounds of dockweed, nettles, coarse grass, and oyster shells, heaped in rank confusion—small dissenting chapels to teach, with no lack of illustration, the miseries of Earth, and plenty of new churches, erected with a little superfluous wealth, to show the way to Heaven. (P. 115)

This is the prose of the crush, of the pollution that results from crowding too many impoverished people into too small an area. The long, long sentence, with its dashes and commas and clauses and lists of city dwellers and their material accoutrements, seems almost to recreate the jumbled, chaotic life of the city itself as the reader struggles through it.

The text resounds too with biblical overtones that evoke the music of death. "This was a wide, wide track"; "'daily bread'"; "new churches . . . to show the way to Heaven." The prose equates the earthly misery it recounts with the path to destruction, the otherworldly promise of Hell for the wicked. It is both a Dickensian and a Victorian trait, indeed, to secularize and make visible and immediate Christian imagery of another world. Perhaps, in an age of doubt, its spokesmen are impatient of a final judgment. Little Nell passes in safety here, however. Her virtue shields her in the passage through this lesser earthly Hell. The section testifies to Nell's status as a symbol, because she remains untainted by the things around her. A realistic character would show more the influences of her surroundings. Nell continues implacably on her self-determined, teleological course, Clarissa-like, to death and repose with her Father in Heaven.

When the two pilgrims find themselves outside London, the text has a visual accompaniment. The illustration (in chapter 15) comments on the prose. The words that carry Nell and her grandfather out of London do so in the same jumbled, vigorous style. Indeed, so crowded is the prose that the reader might easily miss the following reference:

The traveller might stop, and—looking back at Old St. Paul's looming through the smoke, its cross peeping above the crowd (if the day were clear), and glittering in the sun; and casting his eyes upon the Babel out of which it grew until he traced it down to the furthest outposts of the invading army of bricks and mortar whose station lay for the present nearly at his feet— might feel at last that he was clear of London. (P. 116)

What reads like a casual reference to a London landmark assumes much greater importance in the illustration. The "Babel" of London acquires a kind of coherence. It becomes a city of lesser spires dominated by one spire and dome, the tallest of all, St. Paul's. The earthly city of London achieves an iconographical significance when seen from Nell's position of escape. Nell sees that a moral order still does prevail. The city has a point of cohesion, which Nell has discovered, but she has paid an extremely high price. She has traveled through a lesser Hell in her first steps toward what finally proves to be her death. For her, the spire of St. Paul's points teleologically toward her otherworldly home as well.

As Nell leaves London, the quality of the prose abruptly changes. The reader must adjust to a pastoral mode. The long, crowded sentences vanish, replaced by a simpler, almost precious style. Rather than moralistic references to well-known passages from the Bible, the text echoes biblical phrasing for sentimental effect.

> There was a pool of clear water in the field, in which the child laved her hands and face, and cooled her feet before setting forth to walk again. She would have the old man refresh himself in this way, too, and making him sit down upon the grass, cast the water on him with her hands, and dried it with her simple dress. . . .
>
>   He laid his head upon her shoulder and moaned piteously. The time had been, and a very few days before, when the child could not have restrained her tears and must have wept with him. But now she soothed him with gentle and tender words, smiling at his thinking they could ever part, and rallied him cheerfully upon the jest. He was soon calmed and fell asleep, singing to himself in a low voice, like a little child. (P. 117)

Referring to "the child" and "the old man" instead of to Nell and her grandfather, using words like "laved" and "rallied," the conditional tense that imparts an air of ritual, all contribute to the elegiac effect which the biblical rhythm of the words creates.

The peace that Little Nell has found here is the peace of death itself. To be sure, Nell's actual death will come much later, but the long process of dying has begun. We have just stumbled with Nell through a very lively Hell, in sharp contrast with the sweet sterility of the country beyond. Moreover, the narrative mirrors the lifelessness of the pastoral, or perhaps institutes it; the beginning of Nell's death corresponds to the beginning of real difficulties in the prose.

Most readers experience tension as they struggle through these pastoral pages, I think. Their feeling indicates a deeper problem than the mere sentimentality of Dickens's text when it tries to render country scenes. That particular Dickensian failing has attracted its share of critics, but none has paused long enough to remark on the causes of the problem.[9] Now we may see that the sentimental prose signals a structural flaw. The novel has reached an allegorical impasse.

As the ensuing episodes make clear, Little Nell has begun to court death avidly. Her special affinity for the Schoolmaster's favorite pupil, who dies while trying to hold her hand (P. 192), foreshadows broadly her own coming demise. That Nell displays herself in the same cart as one of Mrs. Jarley's wax figures, "decorated with artificial flowers" (P. 216), as if she had already died, suggests again Nell's proximity to death. The reader inevitably comes to associate Nell with her comatose charges. The ludicrous flexibility of the wax dummies, their ability to change, for example, from Mr. Pitt to "the poet Cowper" (P. 216) with a slight switch in costume, parodies the biblical lesson that in death we are all one before God.

Nell's hysterical anxiety lest her grandfather steal from Mrs. Jarley's money box causes the two to flee the quondam security of the show. The flight through the lurid and almost surreal manufacturing town seals Nell's fate. Another journey into Hell, the escape takes Little Nell through a factory where the literal and allegorical levels of the book merge: We are in the fiery pits of eternal suffering. The nameless man who tends the fires has no idea how long he has been doing so; in response to Nell's question, he can only answer, "It has been alive as long as I have" (P. 331). Again, Nell escapes the earthly Hell. Her virtue shields her once more, testifying further to her symbolic durability. She even makes the furnace briefly seem like home, so strong is her allegorical magnetism. She pays a teleological price, however. Struggling for three days in the town, she rises out of her misery by falling into the arms of the Schoolmaster on the third. Like Christ's, her further existence on earth will last only a brief time. Soon she will merge into eternity.

The prefigurations of death in the village at journey's end occur repeatedly. Indeed, they begin in earnest when Nell becomes sick on the trek out of the manufacturing town: "A penny loaf was all they had that day. It was very little, but even hunger was forgotten in the strange tranquility that crept over her senses. She lay down, very gently, and, with a quiet smile on her face, fell into a slumber. It was not like sleep—and yet it must have been, or why those pleasant dreams of the little scholar all night long!" (P. 337). Nell arrives at the town in chapter 46, and we do not witness her further progress until chapter 52, where the intimations of mortality are again everywhere. When introduced to her last earthly home, Nell calls it, "'A quiet, happy place—a place to live and learn to die in!'" (P. 386). The lack of parallelism here emphasizes the oddness of the phrase, coming as it does from a young girl. Or perhaps she is really not so young, as the following passage suggests:

> At that silent hour [late at night], the child lingered before the dying embers, and thought of her past fortunes as if they had been a dream and she only now awoke. The glare of the sinking flame, . . . the aged walls, where strange shadows came and went with every flickering of the fire—the solemn presence, within, of that decay which falls on senseless things . . . : and, without, and round about on every side, of Death—filled her with deep and thoughtful feelings, but with none of terror or alarm. A change had been

gradually stealing over her, in the time of her loneliness and sorrow. With failing strength and heightening resolution, there had sprung up a purified and altered mind; there had grown in her bosom blessed thoughts and hopes, which are the portion of few but the weak and drooping. (P. 388)

We would do well to linger over these sentences, for they tell us something of the narrator's attitude toward death. The confusion over whether Nell dreams or muses while awake introduces a feeling of unreality to the scene. The narrator says, elliptically, that the spooky shadows, which would make a normal person uneasy, do not disturb Nell. Thus the reader realizes that Nell has turned her back on the possibility of life. The "thoughts" that she has do not come to the healthy-minded, but only to the "weak and drooping." Nell associates herself with death and disease. She acts perversely.

The narrator argues implicitly that Nell has a moral duty to live. It is a duty that she abdicates, however. The narrator implies that death belongs to the sick and to the unfit; we pity but do not emulate them. The text does not draw out Little Nell's death, despite the impression that many readers have. After the several chapters of broad hinting about Nell's incipient demise, chapters 52 to 55, the novel does not return to her until chapter 71, when she is already dead. The hiatus of more than one hundred pages no doubt contributes, like the story of Odysseus's scar, to readers' fallacious sense that Nell takes an unduly long time to die. The passages that describe the *reaction* to Nell's death may more justly seem overdone to us, however, because they dwell pitifully on the waste involved. But the text does not wallow in Nell's death. What strikes us modern readers, accustomed to literary restraint, as excessive and thus insincere, is in fact quite sincere in mourning an alarmingly frequent event in the Victorian home.[10] We may charge the narrator with lack of tact in dwelling on grief better left understated. We should realize, however, that our stern analysis derives in large part from our historical and literary vantage points, heirs of a century of novelistic understatement and improved mortality rates.

Death Little Nell has wooed and won. The readers find themselves, I think, wondering why. I have identified Nell as the symbol of the desire for domesticity, the Homeless Angel. The characters in the novel almost instinctively need to surround her with domestic protection. Even the two burly bargemen whom Nell meets while fleeing from her grandfather's imminent theft voice their feeling for her, as immediate and rough as their lives. They break into raucous song. Two less unlikely candidates for domesticity could hardly be found. This extreme example shows how complete is Nell's influence. She embodies, both for the characters and for the reader, the child who needs a parent. More precisely, then, the reader wonders what madness impels this child-goddess to seek death, the antithesis of home and its destroyer.

A child-angel, Nell symbolizes the ideal virtues of the Victorian child.[11] The child should be adoring, simple, and silent. Above all, perhaps, the child should be pure in body and spirit. Little Nell fulfills these great expectations admirably. Her obsessive purity, in fact, becomes so central to her character that, as early as chapter 6, her rejoinder to Quilp's proposal of marriage typifies her response in all her subsequent predicaments:

> "There's no hurry, Little Nell, no hurry at all," said Quilp. "How should you like to be my number two, Nelly? . . . To be Mrs. Quilp the second, when Mrs. Quilp the first is dead, sweet Nell," said Quilp. . . . "Be a good girl, Nelly, a very good girl, and see if one of these days you don't come to be Mrs. Quilp of Tower Hill."
> So far from being sustained and stimulated by this delightful prospect, the child shrunk from him, and trembled. (P. 45)

The narrator's word, "stimulation," which Nell declines in her shrinking person, carries an earthy connotation that shows that the sexual dialogue between Quilp and Nell does not remain at some subconscious level. The text makes explicit symbolic use of moments like this one, creating an allegorical level of meaning. The reader's mental picture of Quilp bending toward Nell while she shrinks away perfectly illustrates that meaning. Nell violently rejects all sexual overtures, just as she rejects any threats to the purity of her being in a larger sense.

Such a pure, beautiful child inevitably attracts offers from characters less scurrilous than Quilp, however. As Nell progresses on her pilgrimage through England, she regularly encounters admirable characters who immediately desire to play father to her child. I have cataloged the host of desiccated old men who surprise their years and us with the strength and quickness of their attachment to Nell. Mrs. Jarley, to be sure, is a woman, but a rather masculine one in the traditional, clichéd sense of the term. She pilots her traveling van and business with a very firm hand. These largely paternal offers, then, represent positive responses to Nell's powerful symbolic presence. But the very responses precipitate an insoluble problem. The relationship between parent and child cannot remain the fixed one for which Nell wishes. The pairing necessarily implies change and violation of that fragile, childish state of innocence. Children grow up to become parents, and parents themselves grow up, away from their children. The temporal, earthly bond between parents and children burdens the child with the necessity of sullying his own timeless, imaginary world with the somber hues of the real.

Nell herself clings, however, to her pure state, rejecting as long as possible the implications of her relationships. She continues instead on her pilgrimage, avoiding permanent connections and seeking a pure Home in which she may remain forever the Child. Out of the tension that her desire creates comes the narrative decision to surround Nell with desiccated old men. They respond hungrily to the symbolic food she offers without apparently demanding any sexual response in return. But the child herself constantly threatens to grow up; she teeters on the brink of sexuality. With the growth that the realistic level of the book demands would come an end to the possibility of an ideal Home that Nell seeks. The realistic and symbolic levels of *The Old Curiosity Shop* clash intolerably here, creating a tension that the text cannot long support. Nell escapes from her parental figures, one after another, but she cannot escape from herself.

Nell thus finds the only remaining solution for the impasse that her demand for a pure Home has created: She wills her own death. In this way, Nell's purity has a teleological dimension. Only in death can she find the Father and the Home for which she longs. Little Nell's superficial fragility barely conceals a fierce desire that exhausts itself maintaining her inviolate state. She demonstrates a great ability to arrange the most untoward circumstances to her domestic benefit. It is in this context that the reader must view Nell's death: her last arrangement.

The narrator makes one final effort to find fertility in the sterile picture that Little Nell's deathbed presents. Repeating a sentiment presented earlier, the passage runs as follows:

> Oh! it is hard to take to heart the lesson that such deaths will teach, but let no man reject it, for it is one that all must learn, and it is a mighty, universal Truth. When Death strikes down the innocent and young, for every fragile form from which he lets the panting spirit free, a hundred virtues rise, in shapes of mercy, charity, and love, to walk the world, and bless it. Of every tear that sorrowing mortals shed on such green graves, some good is born, some gentler nature comes. In the Destroyer's steps there spring up bright creations that defy his power, and his dark path becomes a way of light to Heaven. (P. 544)

If we cannot easily share in the sincerity of the sentiment, excessive as it seems to us, we can now better understand the narrative tensions that produce it, the sexual ambiguities that underlie it, and the real human dilemma that creates the basis for its production.

ii

When the reader first encounters him, Mr. Quilp is following Little Nell into the curiosity shop. Quilp may seem initially like another one of the bizarre objects in the shop, but he quickly emerges from the background as the evil genius of the text:

The child was closely followed by an elderly man of remarkably hard features and forbidding aspect, and so low in stature as to be quite a dwarf. . . . His black eyes were restless, sly, and cunning; his mouth and chin, bristly with the stubble of a coarse hard beard. . . . But what added most to the grotesque expression of his face, was a ghastly smile, which . . . constantly revealed the few discolored fangs that were yet scattered in his mouth, and gave him the aspect of a panting dog. His dress consisted of a large, high-crowned hat, a worn, dark suit, a pair of capacious shoes, and a dirty white neckerchief sufficiently limp and crumpled to disclose the greater portion of his wiry throat. [His] hair . . . was of a grizzled black, . . . and [hung] in a frowzy fringe about his ears. His hands . . . were very dirty; his finger-nails were crooked, long, and yellow. (P. 22)

At this first meeting, however, the reader can only suspect the role that Mr. Quilp will play. He resembles a dog, and a ludicrous one at that, with a few scattered "fangs" and a meaningless smile. The narrator says that Quilp is "elderly," a term that may suggest decrepitude, perhaps, or harmlessness. Soon the reader realizes, however, that Quilp has the energy of a score of younger men and the potential for doing harm of a legion. We almost immediately forget that Quilp would belong to the group of old men who surround Nell, drawn to her symbolic warmth as the Homeless Child, if he were not so energetic and so dangerous. Finally, too, his filthy state appears to indicate want, but the reader soon understands that Quilp's apparent poverty conceals his real wealth and influence among the shadier businessmen of London. At the same time, it reveals his miserliness.

Part of the initial description of Quilp does not mislead the reader. Quilp's hairiness, his large feet (or at least large shoes), his uncovered throat, all traditionally point to sexual potency. Our estimation of Quilp's virility increases as we watch him first with Nell and then with his wife. He must have a perverse sexual charm, we reason, or else no woman, not even one as weak as Mrs. Quilp, would marry him. Our growing realization that Quilp desires a sexual relationship with Nell—even her!—suggests how far the dwarf will go in these matters. He is prodigious.

Nell's reaction to Quilp in their first scene together conveys more than the natural repugnance a child would feel toward a dingy old man with an ugly smile. Nell responds directly to the dwarf's sexual suggestion: "Nell looked at [her grandfather], who nodded to her to retire, and kissed her cheek. 'Ah!' said the dwarf, smacking his lips, 'what a nice kiss that was— just on the rosy part. What a capital kiss!' Nell was none the slower in going away, for this remark. Quilp looked after her with an admiring leer, and when she had closed the door, fell to complimenting the old man on her charms" (P. 72). Nell's physical agility in escaping shows how thoroughly she rejects sexual exchanges. The dwarf's verbal ability in turning a simple kiss into something obscene shows how eagerly he invites them.

The exchanges between Quilp and the old man after Nell's exit reveal much about her grandfather's role in their relationship, as well as about Quilp's character:

> "Such a fresh, blooming, modest little bud, neighbor," said Quilp, nursing his short legs, and making his eyes twinkle very much; "such a chubby, rosy, cosy, Little Nell!"
>
> The old man answered by a forced smile, and was plainly struggling with a feeling of the keenest and most exquisite impatience. It was not lost upon Quilp, who delighted in torturing him, or indeed anybody else, when he could.
>
> "She's so," said Quilp, speaking very slowly, and feigning to be quite absorbed in the subject, "so small, so compact, so beautifully modelled, so fair, with such blue veins and such a transparent skin, and such little feet, and such winning ways—but bless me, you're nervous!" (P. 73)

Nell's grandfather evinces extreme discomfort because he wishes to act as a perpetual father to Nell. Quilp's physical appreciation of her disturbs the old man as it reminds him that Nell is a sexual being in some sense and that she will soon become a woman. The old man maintains a fragile emotional balance between fear of Quilp the moneylender and love for an image of Little Nell.

In Quilp's glee at the old man's discomfort, and in the very strength and linguistic excess of the dwarf's improbable lust for Nell, the reader witnesses the extreme quality of Quilp's character. While Nell fervently seeks to escape life, the dwarf embraces it, wickedly, as long as all goes according to his plan. As long as the dwarf succeeds in his evil scheming, in other words, life seems to him "rosy, cosy." He glories in living, he lives ardently, greedily. Indeed, George Bataille defines eroticism as assenting to life up to the point of death. In this sense, Quilp is as erotic as Nell is not.[12]

The monstrous Quilp rapidly becomes for the reader a demon of evil, of eroticism, of excess, of energy. During Nell's temporary stay at the waxworks in chapter 27, she has an illustrative encounter with Quilp: "there suddenly emerged from the black shade of the arch, a man. The instant he appeared, she recognized him. Who could have failed to recognize, in that instant, the ugly, mis-shapen Quilp! . . . He seemed to have risen out of the earth" (P. 207). Nell's thoughts appear to conjure up the demon Quilp. He rises "out of the earth," acquiring a Satanic aura; he can apparently take any shape he wills, so "misshapen" is he. The accompanying illustration further heightens our impression. Nell crouches near a niche containing a tiny saint, or Madonna, while Quilp, with his aggressive stance and his stick, identifies himself with the fierce grotesques in the bridge above. For the other characters and for the reader, Quilp becomes a prodigious Imp of potential wickedness. Kit responds to him, for instance, as if an evil omen had suddenly taken human form and desired to trouble him. Both Kit and his mother are often struck with mental paralysis on seeing Quilp; their attitudes testify to his symbolic potency. When Mrs. Nubbles rides back to London inside the coach with Quilp leering down at her from above, she finds his iconographic purport completely unnerving and is reduced to near idiocy by the time she arrives in London.

Quilp's drinking and other feats of physical excess work powerfully on Dick Swiveller and Sampson Brass to induce a similar attitude toward the dwarf in these two legal gentlemen. In chapter 11, Quilp smokes both to inure himself to the old man's infection and to torment Brass. Brass begins to doubt, indeed, the terrestrial origin of Quilp, who smokes without surcease and orders Brass and the boy to do the same. Quilp's drinking of boiling spirits has an even more profound effect on the men and the reader too. Swiveller, no mean bibber himself, asks in astonishment, "'Why, man, you don't mean to tell me that you drink such fire as this?'" (P. 163). Brass, conditioned by long experience to respond with servile pleasantries to anything that Quilp does or says, manages to choke out, "'Oh very biting! and yet it's like being tickled—there's a pleasure in it too, sir!'" (P. 463). Dickens continues: "The wretched Sampson took a few short sips of the liquor, which immediately distilled itself into burning tears, . . . turning the colour of his face and eyelids to a deep red, and giving rise to a violent fit of coughing, in the midst of which he was still heard to declare, with the constancy of a martyr, that it was 'beautiful indeed!'" (P. 463). Episodes like these create in the characters' minds and in the reader's a sense of Quilp as an inspired demon. His brilliance lies in no small way in his strenuous excess in matters both large and small. The illustration in chapter 60 (opp. P. 447) shows Quilp leering down at Kit out of a window in the dwarf's moment of triumph, with a sign reading, "Man . . . Beast" on the wall beside. At that moment, if not before, both characters and reader must seriously wonder from what satanic source Quilp derives his evil energies.[13]

Questions arise in the reader's mind, however, about the limits to this demon's powers. We begin to wonder what the Man-Beast specifically wants, because his choice of a particular object for his hatred will restrict and focus his energies. What Quilp rejects and what he chooses will both determine his fate in the text and identify his symbolic presence more precisely in the reader's mind.

In chapter 21, Quilp reveals to the reader in a Shakespearean monologue what he intends to perpetrate in the next few chapters. Quilp "throw[s] himself on the ground," and "scream[s] and roll[s] about in uncontrollable delight," thus indicating his relish of anticipated villainy (P. 164). He confides to the reader that, by promoting the marriage of Dick Swiveller and Little Nell

under the former's false expectations of a rich dowry, Quilp will have a
"clearing of old scores." Among these old scores, he tells us, are Mr. Trent's
"ma[king] eyes at Mrs. Quilp," as well as Swiveller's "ma[king] his bones
ache t'other day" (P. 164). But the reader does not seriously believe that
Swiveller will marry Nell. Dick has an ultimately comic part to play in the
novel. Further, Quilp's motivation seems petty, so far beneath Nell's concerns as to appear ineffectual against her progress toward an other worldly
home. Quilp signals his pettiness and impotence, I think, with his "uncontrollable" frenzy of mean exultation. The villain in the piece, like Richard
III, impresses us with his power only so long as he controls himself first and
the situation second. As soon as he loses control of himself, we sense that
loss of control over the situation must inevitably follow.

At the end of the chapter, the narrator adds a revealing scene that catches exactly the quality of Quilp's passion:

> In the height of his ecstasy, Mr. Quilp had like to have met with a disagree-
> able check, for rolling very near a broken dog-kennel, there leapt forth a
> large fierce dog, who, but that his chain was of the shortest, would have
> given him a disagreeable salute. As it was, the dwarf remained upon his
> back in perfect safety. . . .
>
> "Why don't you come and bite me, why don't you come and tear me to
> pieces, you coward?" said Quilp, hissing and worrying the animal till he was
> nearly mad. "You're afraid, you bully, you're afraid, you know you are."
>
> The dog tore and strained at his chain . . . , but there the dwarf lay, snap-
> ping his fingers with gestures of defiance and contempt. (Pp. 164-65)

In a very few words, the narrator delineates the barely restrained ferocity that
drives Quilp in his petty scheming. Because he detests everything, one object
is as satisfactory as another for his wrath. Thus he picks the one nearest to
hand—his revenge must be convenient. Part of his delight derives from the
ease with which he achieves his villainous goal. Further, the victim must not
be able to retaliate. A chained dog, like a cowed wife, works very well; Quilp
stays just out of reach of the snapping fangs. The moment perfectly captures
the spirit in which Quilp plots to make Kit and Nell miserable. He chooses
characters who seem to possess no means of revenge. That he overreaches
himself, underestimating the more powerful characters' desire to protect Nell
and Kit, testifies at once to his greed and to an ultimate weakness in his nature.

Quilp's own words reveal more than he intends. He thinks that he taunts
an enraged, helpless dog, but in fact he describes his own character. "'You're
afraid, you bully, you're afraid, you know you are.'" Quilp himself is
afraid—afraid of the savagery of his own nature, afraid of the anger of others. The dog mirrors Quilp in the barely restrained frustration and rage
that permeates his being.

At the moment of the dwarf's apparent petty triumph over Kit, then, when Quilp leans out of the window leering like a "Man-Beast," the reader's sense of the strength of the demon locked within Quilp's stunted body is tempered by a concomitant suspicion that he has wasted his huge if wicked talent on the wrong objects. We think of Kit as a sort of divine idiot and do not fear that any permanent harm will come to him. Quilp passionately spends his prodigious capital of evil energy on unworkable ventures. The paradox here is that a powerfully corrupt being finds that the apparently weak in fact possess the endless strength of those who can sink no lower. It is an example of the inability of evil finally to prevail over good in the traditional novelistic world. *The Old Curiosity Shop* endorses the comfortable teleological hierarchy, common to other ages besides the Victorian, of right over wrong. Nell's purity leads her surely to Heaven and Quilp's pure malice drives him inexorably to oblivion. The novel leaves readers with a more difficult conundrum to solve, however, than the simple one of giving each character his just deserts. Readers must explain to themselves the strange presence of a demon like Quilp in the first place. In *The Old Curiosity Shop*, evil seems intrusive and unexplained.[14]

We may now define Quilp's role in the novel in opposition to Nell more precisely, I think. Just as Nell acquires solicitous parental figures, Quilp collects seedy characters from the world of work. His lust to wreak evil on the living rages as strongly as does Nell's desire for purity and death. The other characters group themselves around these two, one judging life and finding it morally inadequate, the other savagely exploiting it in an attempt to assuage the unassuageable hurts life has given him. Quilp's love of life involves rejection, so close is it to hate. For characters radically dissimilar yet joined in their passionate response to life to reject the world leaves the reader in the middle wondering where to turn when either purity or corruption leads to death.[15]

Nell and Quilp represent poles of sexual energy. Nell sublimates hers and exhausts it in death. Quilp expends his energy in terrorizing his wife, Mrs. Jiniwin, and the other women in their circle, as well as Nell herself. Further, he exhausts his excess passion on his business dealings, taking the reader willy-nilly on an archaeological exploration of sordid motivation and mean dealing in the nether world of Victorian finance. Like a nineteenth-century Richard III, Quilp compels us with his wicked enthusiasm to become his accomplices on the voyage. Quilp bridges the gulf between home and work when he abandons his wife after his presumed death and takes up a tatterdemalion bachelor life in the countinghouse. Thus the text links Work and Home along the chain of desire that binds Nell at one end and Quilp at the other.

Our estimation of Quilp's physical and moral ugliness heightens our wonder at his ability to fascinate the women in his wife's circle. He titillates these ladies at least, if he does not quite compel their admiration. Similarly, such is his forceful, consuming personality that Quilp draws loyalty from the most unpromising material, Mr. Sampson Brass and his sister Sally. Further, the Marchioness may owe her existence to the union of Sally and Quilp. The narrator hints at the possibility when Quilp takes an unusual interest in the child (P. 380) and when the narrator makes an ironic reference to Miss Brass's virginity in chapter 36, remarking that "some extraordinary grudge" must provoke her otherwise inexplicably cruel treatment of the small servant (P. 273). These moments point to morally obscure regions at the edges of the reader's novelistic awareness. Readers engage in an archaeology, then, with no certain bounds; they see the moral ground fast disappearing under their literary excavations with no assurance that the limits of evil in *The Old Curiosity Shop* can ever be found.

Quilp's establishment of bachelor quarters suggests a kind of limit to his passionate nature. He yields to the need to create a temporary home. His gesture aligns him with two other characters in the novel: the Lodger (with his marvelous kit) and Mrs. Jarley (with her cozy caravan). It is an interesting group. The three characters share a domestic interest in Nell. The Lodger's temporary digs give him a position from which he may investigate the Punch and Judy shows that he hopes will lead him to Nell. Mrs. Jarley's decision to take Nell under her corpulent corporate wing grows out of her outraged sense of parenthood. She is irritated by the disparity between her obvious comfort in the caravan and Nell's palpable poverty outside. Finally, Quilp's chase after Nell begins a chain of events that leads to his moving into the countinghouse.

The temporary nature of these characters' solutions to the domestic problem posed by the advent of Nell into their lives parallels her status as pilgrim. Not only does she wander the face of England herself, but she sets in motion the characters whose lives she touches as well. That Quilp joins the pilgrims shows how effectively the weak Angel puts the evil Imp to rout. Quilp attempts to interfere with Nell's life precisely because the two represent opposite poles in the symbolism of the novel. Young, beautiful, and good, Little Nell by her very presence antagonizes the old, ugly, and evil Quilp. Quilp thinks that if he can manipulate Nell into marrying him, he may change her. To change Nell is to corrupt her, to take her out of the angelic host, to make her more endurable to one as fallen as Quilp himself.

Modern readers find themselves admiring Quilp in a limited way here, I think. Quilp possesses a great ability to control the chaotic life of the city that swirls unceasingly around him. He dances ecstatically amid the mayhem of urban life, delighting in his ability to manipulate a part of it, and the performance fascinates us. At the same time, too, we detest him. He corrupts everything within his grasp. Quilp even tries to commit the unspeakably low act of marrying Nell. Our sense of Quilp's unsuitability for Nell leads us to a more disturbing realization, however. Nell loses our esteem as she takes one life-denying step after another. As Nell leaves us behind, though, we are lost; we do not know to whom to transfer our sympathies. We hate Quilp for forcing us to see how far from the angels and how close to the devils our sympathies actually lie. Quilp disturbs us because he strips away our own easy pretenses to morality even as we reject him. We do so too late in our reading to remain comfortable in naïve moral rectitude.

Quilp represents not only the best commentary the novel offers us on Nell but also the most damning commentary on ourselves. The text pushes these characters toward extreme good and evil. Although we may in the end reject such a polarization as overly simplistic, nonetheless that reflection occurs only after the text has tricked us into siding temporarily with the devils. We have the freedom to pick up the novel or not, but once we have decided to read it, it severely curtails our choices, among them our choice of characters with whom we may identify.[16] Reading *The Old Curiosity Shop* brings about a self-betrayal in a literal sense. It forces on readers choices they cannot comfortably make.

Quilp pairs with another character in the novel as well. The frowning mask of his face reminds the reader of Kit's laughing gargoyle face, described in the first chapters of the novel. When Quilp beats the figurehead that he identifies as Kit in a weird voodoolike rite in chapter 62, the feeling in the air is like that of a sick room. Quilp's mad enthusiasm infects us uncomfortably. The passage makes us wonder why he loves to hate Kit so much, why he joins himself with Kit in such an odd relationship.

We may cite superficial reasons of the sort that Quilp himself invokes in his more confiding moments. Kit has interfered with his plans, Kit has a special fondness for Nell, and so on. But a deeper motivation lies beneath these convenient explanations. Quilp hates Kit because he periodically tells Quilp quite frankly what he thinks of the dwarf and how the misshapen creature looks to him. None of the conventional restraints of social intercourse keeps a holy fool like Kit from speaking his simple mind. Kit sees Quilp clearly in all his moral ugliness; Quilp does not impress him in the least. Thus Kit holds up to Quilp's unwilling eyes a mirror to the ethical emptiness of his soul, and the dwarf shrinks from the reflection, hating Kit for showing it to him. All the other characters except one restrain themselves out of fear or even pity from speaking frankly to Quilp.

Tom Scott, the lad who inhabits Quilp's wharf, is the exception. He regularly calls Quilp a monster but in a different way from Kit. Tom Scott loves his master, and his insults really convey a gruff affection that the shrewd Quilp does not fail to catch. He tolerates Tom's abuse, giving plenty in return, because of the odd companionship that the relationship affords.

Sadism is the only medium by which these two emotional outcasts may express their mutual affection.

In chapter 49, Quilp returns from the dead, much to the chagrin of his erstwhile family circle. In doing so, he demonstrates an important part of his hold on us. He has conquered mortality in a figurative sense, proving once again his ability to control any situation. In his prodigious tippling, his tireless smoking, his attempts to control the other characters, and his other feats of demonic strength, Quilp evinces an ability to manipulate people and events that foreshadows his most spectacular manipulation in chapter 49. Quilp's mania for power covers at its root a desperate desire to control his own mortality in a genuine sense. The novel only permits him a figurative control, but the scene conjures up more ominous shadows. It troubles us because of the suggestions it makes about Quilp's powers. It asks, in effect, whether or not he may prove genuinely indomitable as he has figuratively. The text reassures the harried reader who entertains such dispiriting notions, however, through the actions of Tom Scott.

The lad witnesses from the beginning Quilp's return. The two conspire to surprise Quilp's mourning family and friends: Quilp will eavesdrop on the assembled group, thrusting himself on them at the precise moment of their supreme embarrassment. The two conspirators hardly exchange any words at all. They do not need to, because they think alike under such circumstances. "They both stood for some seconds, grinning and gasping and wagging their heads at each other, on either side of the post, like an unmatchable pair of Chinese idols" (P. 365). Quilp's boyish delight in their scurrilous play brings the man down to the size of the lad in our eyes. Here we have no master of evil, the reader realizes, only an old imp who cannot help taking advantage of an easy chance to cause discomfort to his associates. Such a petty creature could not really live forever or even outlast the narrative. Indeed, as subsequent events make us realize, Quilp does die in a sense during his absence. Upon his return, he has already taken the first of a series of steps toward death, away from the circle of the living from whom he has drawn his energy.

The night of Quilp's return he spends tormenting Mrs. Quilp. It is their last night together, surprisingly enough to the genuine sorrow of Mrs. Quilp, though her regret is not unmixed with relief. Quilp becomes a bachelor, withdrawing to the solitary life of his countinghouse. He takes only Tom Scott with him. Certainly, Quilp has not exhausted his activities in the business realm at this stage of the narrative. He has removed himself from even a semblance of Victorian family life, however, and such a step represents a first one toward nonexistence. Quilp polarizes himself, in effect; he cuts himself off from the source of much of his spite. The dwarf becomes a money-hungry schemer, losing his sense of fun. Quilp never realizes how much he needs Mrs. Jiniwin and his wife to draw energy from in vampirelike fashion.

Thus Quilp's remove to the countinghouse becomes important to the symbolic level of the novel as it suggests that the two symbolic poles, Nell and Quilp, participate in each other's realm of meaning. Much of Quilp's delight in his own villainy he both derives from and renews at the fount of nefarious opportunity his home presents. In a similar fashion, Nell derives her determination to persevere in her pilgrimage not only from her pure love of the simple life (and death) but also from an antipathetic curiosity about the pelf that has corrupted her grandfather. One thinks in this context of her horrified enthrallment while witnessing her grandfather's thievery late one night at the inn in chapter 30.

Toward the end of his life, Quilp becomes increasingly acerb and vicious, and even his most faithful business partners avoid him. Sampson Brass, not wanting to be the very last rat to leave the ship, abandons Quilp principally out of cowardice but also out of a sense that Quilp has finally lost the ability to conspire effectively during his bachelorhood. Sampson shows his disaffection when he questions Quilp's judgment in shrieking so loudly the particulars of his late triumph over Kit even in a spot as forsaken as the countinghouse. It is the first time that Brass has dared to question Quilp's judgment. The conventional Sampson fears the dwarf's apparent irrationality. For a weasel like Brass, defection cannot be far off after such an open break with the commander in chief.

Increasingly bitter in his isolation, Quilp resorts to more and more bizarre behavior, such as striking the figurehead in a grisly sort of ritual and going to the "summer-house" for an "unusual, unsophisticated, primitive" picnic (P. 381). Finally, evil energy cannot replace the fruitful love that the text preaches every human being must show in good works and that Quilp unequivocally lacks. Our delight with the creative aspects of Quilp's evil genius—his potential for wreaking ingenious harm on those less adept in plotting than he—must end with the realization that Quilp's impulses will inevitably destroy him.

Even the sadistic but genuine love that Quilp and Tom Scott have for one another does not finally bear any fruit. Tom as a character has no existence apart from the dwarf. Tom is Quilp's creature; we only find him in the text when Quilp appears. Tom belongs completely to the milieu of Quilp's wharf. Without Quilp both the wharf and Tom will sink into oblivion. Tom will disappear, indeed, like one of the amphibious creatures to which the narrator has compared him throughout the story. When Quilp withdraws to his countinghouse for the last time, then, his withdrawal from humanity becomes complete despite Tom's presence. The lad merely functions as Quilp's reflection, or rather as a pair of heels for Quilp's hands (such as in their sadistic games). Just before his death, Quilp sends Tom away. Because of their need for each other, the reader must see Quilp's action as the second step in a virtual suicide:

> He stood listening intently, but the noise [of his pursuers] was not renewed. Nothing was to be heard in that deserted place, but, at intervals, the distant barking of the dogs. The sound was far away—now in one quarter, now answered in another—nor was it any guide, for it often came from ship-board, as he knew.
>
> "If I could find a wall or fence," said the dwarf, stretching out his arms, and walking slowly on, "I should know which way to turn. A good, black, devil's night this, to have my dear friend [Brass] here! If I had but that wish, it might, for anything I cared, never be day again." (Pp. 509–10)

Quilp gets that suicidal wish almost as he speaks, and the event indicates to the reader how far from his earlier evil exultation Quilp has come. He tumbles into the water of the Thames and drowns, fighting grimly, without the buoyancy of his earlier career. "Another mortal struggle, and he was up again, beating the water with his hands, and looking out, with wild and glaring eyes. . . . One loud cry now—but the resistless water bore him down before he could give it utterance, and, driving him under it, carried away a corpse" (P. 510). The word "resistless" could apply in its different senses both to Quilp and to the water. His last attempts to control the events that swirl around him shows all the other attempts ultimately to be as futile as this one. Without love, the novel tells us, even the most vigorous and ingenious of characters must leave the world with empty hands.

iii

Quilp's virtual suicide underscores the connections between the dwarf and Little Nell on both the symbolic and the narrative levels of the text. In a symbolic sense, Nell and Quilp mirror each other at opposite ends of the spectrum of desire, the former wishing for a pure existence with her heavenly Father, and the latter seeking to gratify earthly passions in the city of man. Not least among his desires is the wish to possess the body of an angel. In a narrative sense, Nell and Quilp provide the motivation for much of the rest of the characters' activities. It seems the more remarkable, then, that Nell and Quilp should both die as quickly as they do. Quilp drowns several chapters before the end of *The Old Curiosity Shop,* and Nell drops out of the story nineteen chapters before the end. When we return to the village in the last chapters, she has already died. The reader may well wonder why the narrative requires such an extended coda. Further, we may ask how these early departures serve the symbolic content of the novel, when so much of it depends on Nell and Quilp and their battle for the reader's sympathies.

The *telos* of Nell's pure desire proves to be death, with a heaven dimly felt beyond. Her demise has its greatest effect on earth, where a "hundred virtues" rise from her grave. The *arche* of desire seems to be death as well; Quilp's political and sexual scheming leads him inexorably to his last misstep on the pier, a misstep that sends him to a death by water. So strong is Quilp's self-hatred, finally, that it destroys him. All his machinations come to nothing. A finite evil being spends himself in attempting to conquer the infinite goodwill of the novel. The story leaves the reader deprived, then, of the two extremes of possible response to the demands that a morally murky world makes on us. The reader must find a middle course, a secularized posture that avoids the self-induced death that takes the absolutely pure and absolutely corrupt alike. *The Old Curiosity Shop* points the reader toward an earthly reality among the humbler characters who remain after Nell and Quilp have torn themselves out of the novel. Thus the polarization of readers' sympathies ultimately directs them back to the prosaic world, away from the demonic, away from the otherworldly.

Nell's death makes the humble marriage of Kit and Barbara possible in ways both literal and symbolic. Nell represents to Kit something more than human and less than divine: an image of the pure woman. Kit pledges himself to her first, making subsequent marriage to Barbara difficult. It is only as he leaves Barbara to see Nell for the last time that Kit clears the air, removing the twin obstacles of his symbolic hero worship and Barbara's literal, earthly jealousy. The brood of children that quickly appears around the feet of Kit and Barbara becomes, then, the legacy of Nell's death and provides at least four of the "hundred virtues" that the novel mentions. On the symbolic level, Nell's pure sterility would have precluded such progeny. *The Old Curiosity Shop* implicitly recognizes the need to replace Nell as a symbolic presence with a prolific family.

Another pair prospers as well after the deaths of Nell and Quilp. Dick Swiveller and the Marchionness become the representatives of a more exalted class of secular survivors, because Dick's inherited wealth makes work unnecessary. The novel does not mention any offspring; if Quilp and Sally Brass are indeed her parents, the Marchionness's children would have too monstrous a lineage. Quilp's death in part wipes the moral slate of the novel clean. If *The Old Curiosity Shop* is to show evil to be an empty thing, all traces of Quilp must vanish from the reclaimed, secular city.[17]

At the end of the novel, then, the city does seem cleansed, with a proper moral perspective restored. But to achieve that impression, the novel must focus in the last several chapters on a very restricted image indeed. Nell's journey through the manufacturing hell does not stop troubling the reader's mind even though she has reached happier places. The nameless worker in the furnace must tend the fires still. The poor, the sick, and the unwanted remain; the pilgrim's vision of them has not been exorcised as Quilp has. Although the novel has shown Quilp's evil to be self-destructive, it has not demonstrated that any other villains will annihilate themselves. Mention of the gamblers and Frederick Trent in the last chapter reminds the reader that Quilp's nefarious confederates still roam the streets. Sampson and Sally become wandering ghouls who trespass on the just peace of the city as "the embodied spirits of Disease, and Vice, and Famine" (P. 549). Quilp, who was a demon of evil, has become a mere body about which an inquest can be held, while Sampson and Sally, who were prosaic thieves, have become walking demons. Thus the text attempts to denature evil in the restricted world in which the Nubbles and the Swivellers, the Garlands, and the Abel Garlands live. But in the larger circle of London, as the novel admits, evil has not been rendered harmless.

The new city has its isolated gardens. The Swivellers' Hampstead smoking box, the Nubbles' home, the Garlands' cottage—in these oases the story attempts to resolve the tensions that Nell and Quilp have engendered. The earthly sanctity of the home, the beneficent use of money, and the proper role of work find a balance of sorts here in these sheltered, bourgeois castles. Mr. Garland makes a living in his largely unspecified business only to come home to his quaint cottage and quaint wife. The last chapter records in so many words that Kit becomes prosperous at his work, but it dwells on his children and the Pony. Swiveller does not work at all. The rapacious world of business that Quilp represents, in short, is accepted in *The Old Curiosity Shop* only when put in a perspective that includes the softening influences of a home redolent with the Victorian values of a large family and the physical comforts prosperity can bring. The modern reader's ambivalence toward the resolution of *The Old Curiosity Shop* stems from the undeniable attraction of these peaceful havens on the one hand and from the suspicion on the other hand that they represent a mere withdrawal from, not a solution to, the difficult realities of urban life. The symbolic heat of the world of work that Quilp has wickedly embodied further contributes to our ambivalence, because these domestic retreats must seem tepid, if morally correct, in comparison.

The text has perhaps a final, unsentimental communication to make. In the relationship between Quilp and Tom Scott, the reader finds a genuine, if sadistic, affection. Between Codlin and Short a similar bond of real but rough-edged love exists. Mrs. Jarley, so stolid and paternal a proprietor, manages nonetheless to link herself to "the philosophical George" (P. 352). When justice falls on them, it finds Sally and Sampson wandering together; similarly, List and Jowl find the criminal life more tolerable in company than apart. So sustaining are these relationships for the characters who create them that one senses Quilp himself might have survived had he not systematically sent his friends away. Nell and her grandfather, the archetypal pair of pilgrims, demonstrate on every page their mutual need. Betrayal weakens but rarely breaks the bonds of companionship between Nell and her grandfather, and those of the other characters in the story. The novel shows the reader the necessary conditions for and the possibilities of these units of human meaning in which social relations begin. *The Old Curiosity Shop* testifies both to the durability and the importance of human community. In the companionship of these pairs of characters, we may find evidence for a continuity from the Victorian world to our own, and from one moment in the helter-skelter present to the next.

Uriah Heep
David Copperfield

3

Doric Dreams

Nine days I drifted on the teeming sea
before dangerous high winds. Upon the tenth
we came to the coastline of the Lotos Eaters,
who live upon that flower. We landed there
to take on water. All ships' companies
mustered alongside for the mid-day meal.
Then I sent out two picked men and a runner
to learn what race of men that land sustained.
They fell in, soon enough, with Lotos Eaters,
who showed no will to do us harm, only
offering the sweet Lotos to our friends—
but those who ate this honeyed plant, the Lotos,
never cared to report, nor to return:
they longed to stay forever, browsing on
that native bloom, forgetful of their homeland.

Homer, Odyssey 9.83–97

David Copperfield gives the reader a more limited choice of identification than *The Old Curiosity Shop*, for it forces the reader to witness the events in the novel from the hero's point of view. We never get to consider David Copperfield's world from Uriah's perspective, for instance, or Mr. Murdstone's, or even that of the man who cries "goroo, goroo," at David on his trip to Dover.[1] That humble merchant derives what life he has from David's fairy-tale idea of him as an ogre. Indeed, for David as well as for the reader, the proprietor of the junk shop is a character in a book. In reading *David Copperfield*, we must look through David's eyes, or we cannot see at all.[2] The key to understanding *David Copperfield*, therefore, is understanding what David Copperfield wants.

In *David Copperfield*, as in first-person fiction in general, the narrator risks alienating his readers by abusing the power he holds over them, indulging in the novelistic gratification of his private desires at the expense of believability—and the reader's patience. David frequently threatens to blur the distinctions between dreams and reality, excess and restraint, in his own life story. In *The Old Curiosity Shop*, Nell rejects the living world for a pure death. Reading *David Copperfield*, we wonder in turn whether David can maintain a rational view of the world even as he narrates the riotous desires of his dreams.

Critics of *David Copperfield* must first of all grapple with this narrative voice. We have a right to be suspicious initially; what we are reading is literally an imposition. We must not, then, give in too easily to David's seductively plausible voice. He discusses his self-appointed task at several places in the novel. For example, he writes "In fulfillment of the compact I have made with myself, to reflect my mind on this paper, I again examine it, closely, and bring its secrets to light" (P. 697). Further, "This manuscript is intended for no eyes but mine" (P. 606). Finally, the opening of the novel, "Whether I shall turn out to be the hero of my own life, or whether that station will be held by anybody else, these pages must show" (P. 1).

The quotations reveal the narrator's uncertainty concerning the confessional nature of first-person fiction, as well as his apparent uncertainty in the beginning about exactly what he will disclose. I think the contradictions here show a real discomfort over the possible extent of his revelations. In effect, the narrator implicitly raises the very real possibility—in fact, the certainty—that he will lie to us. The ambiguity in these several statements about the private communications the reader will confront points up some of the tensions inherent in first-person fiction. The reader must accept a greater intimacy than with other literary forms. Here, we may encounter the justifications, the confessions, even the self-serving lies that an individual employs to carry on in an ethically uncertain world. At the same time, such a narrative possesses a potentially great appeal. Through comparison of our own memories with those of the narrator, we may develop concurrent images of the hero and of ourselves. Comparing the two images may educate, relieve, or dismay us. A first-person narrative offers special opportunities for such study because it can follow the fortune of one particular character more completely than other forms can. More specifically, the reader may learn about one character's psyche in more intimate detail than from any other form.

The few comments that David makes about his story should alert us, however, to the limitations within which a first-person narrative works. The other characters derive their very existence from the hero. Their vitality as individual beings depends on the narrator's ability to enter into the souls of other human beings and to reproduce what he finds in prose. The narrator is much larger than his narrative.

Every person, or persona, tends to choose the companions of his youth and maturity from those who remind him, in some aspect, consciously or unconsciously, of the important figures of his childhood.[3] Thus, the people with whom we form relationships after we have left childhood at times represent doubles of primal roles. To be sure, the healthy among us develop and change, leaving much of the past behind in our psychic graveyards. But few of us indeed can claim to have no ghosts at all haunting our psyches. More often than not, we befriend similar sorts of people habitually in an unconscious effort to make a perfect relationship in the place of a sadly imperfect one with a parent, a sibling, or the like.[4]

For David, the cast of characters of *David Copperfield* comes to resemble the resident troupe of a European opera house, with the differing roles played by the same versatile actors and actresses. Thus, if we can identify the principal players, we will have well begun understanding David, and thus *David Copperfield.*

Our re-creation of *David Copperfield*, then, will develop from our understanding of David's psyche, leading to a sense of the text as a whole. In the process, we will also enlarge our understanding of the constraints inherent to reading, limited as it is by each reader's capacity to imagine a fictive world in terms of his own psychic cast of characters. For our argument implies that just as each person tends to select among the people he meets those who seem familiar to him in some sense, each *reader* responds to *reading* in a similarly directed way.[5] Our ability to assimilate the utterly new is limited by our tendency to hold jealously to past knowledge and experience, and to open our arms to receive the future with a certain reluctance, like children, afraid of the unmet.

The narrator's comments about writing down his "secrets" suggest that he attempts a self-analysis. He performs his own archaeological search in an effort to unearth the buried mysteries of his "undisciplined heart" (P. 768) in order to comprehend what causes the unease that torments him for so long: "The old unhappy feeling pervaded my life. . . . I loved my wife [Dora] dearly, and I was happy; but the happiness I had vaguely anticipated, once, was not the happiness I enjoyed, and there was always something wanting" (P. 697).[6]

At the same time, however, the narrator creates a teleology out of David's efforts at self-understanding. As he muses over the events of his life, he selects those that have meaning for him; he develops his own personal mythology. The process shows itself most clearly at moments such as the one at the end of the novel, when David self-consciously looks to Agnes, "pointing upward," for the inspiration that enables him to go from day to day in his novelistic career (P. 877).

Late in the novel, David describes his memories of his long period of depression following Dora's death.

> There are some dreams that can only be imperfectly described; and when
> I oblige myself to look back on this time of my life, I seem to be recalling
> such a dream. I see myself passing on among the novelties of foreign towns,
> palaces, cathedrals, temples, pictures, castles, tombs, fantastic streets—the
> old abiding places of History and Fancy—as a dreamer might; bearing my
> painful load through it all, and hardly conscious of the objects as they fade
> before me. Listlessness to everything, but brooding sorrow, was the night
> that fell on my undisciplined heart. Let me look up from it—as at last I did,
> thank Heaven!—and from its long, sad, wretched dream, to dawn. (P. 814)

The particular form his musing takes demands special attention. He says that
he acts like a dreamer, "hardly conscious" of the endless succession of "towns,
palaces, cathedrals" that he has visited in a forlorn attempt to find diversion.
But readers must recall as they read this passage that David married Dora in
precisely the same terms. That too seemed like a dream, especially at first:

> The church is calm enough, I am sure; but it might be a steam-power loom
> in full action, for any sedative effect it has on me. I am too far gone for that.
>   The rest is all a more or less incoherent dream.
>   A dream of their coming in with Dora; of the pew-opener arranging us,
> like a drill-sergeant, before the altar rails; of my wondering, even then, why
> pew-openers must always be the most disagreeable females procurable, and
> whether there is any religious dread of a disastrous infection of good humour
> which renders it indispensable to set those vessels of vinegar upon the road
> to Heaven.
>   Of the clergyman and clerk appearing; of a few boatmen and some other
> people strolling in. . . . (P. 631)

The succession of prepositional phrases adds to the disjointed effect the present tense creates here. Marriage to Dora, it seems, begins and ends in a dream.

Apparently, the narrator wishes simply to stress the fairy-tale aspect of
David's union with Dora, to show how wrongheaded their marriage proves
to be for both. If readers connect the scene with others throughout the text,
however, they will realize that the narrator unwittingly suggests a subtler
point here as well. Dream and "Fancy" (P. 13) work thematically at the
center of the narrative, instructing the reader about the state of David's
psychic development throughout the story. As we begin to know David,
we realize that he fights a dialectical battle within himself, pitting David
the dreamer against David the self-disciplined worker. The self-indulgence
that tempts a first-person narrator in general, then, finds particular expression in this tale of fancy, *David Copperfield.*

i

The opening of the novel details, in often playful prose, the idyllic and painful experiences of David's childhood. Critics have tended to remark on the section as if it neatly separated itself from the rest of the novel, an inspired evocation of childhood from the child's point of view.[7] But in fact, the first section establishes several remarkable character types who will reappear in different guises throughout the remainder of the story. Manipulative women, malleable men, the Murdstone type, those who protect David with their love, and those who cannot, fill the pages of *David Copperfield.* I begin by sketching the types important in David's early life.

David remembers that he was born with a "caul," which gives rise to the predictions of the nurse and "some sage women in the neighborhood" (P. 1) that David will possess powers of sight far beyond the ordinary. He further remembers that:

> The caul was won [in a raffle] by an old lady with a handbasket. . . . She had never been on the water in her life . . . ; and . . . over her tea (to which she was extremely partial) she, to the last, expressed her indignation at the impiety of mariners and others, who had the presumption to go "meandering" about the world. It was in vain to represent to her that some conveniences, tea perhaps included, resulted from this objectionable practice. She always returned, with greater emphasis and with an instinctive knowledge of the strength of her objection, "Let us have no meandering." (P. 2)

This remarkable woman possesses two salient characteristics: her age and her obstinacy. She prefigures two more important characters in the book. She will become on the one hand Miss Murdstone and on the other hand Betsy Trotwood, David's aunt. Both prove themselves to be equally inflexible, and both live largely on the strength of their wills. Miss Murdstone represents, however, the evil form that such a character might take, while Miss Trotwood represents in her turn the good. Miss Murdstone and David's aunt differ in their capacity for giving and receiving love from others. Miss Murdstone, far more than Miss Trotwood, acts like "the discontented fairy . . . [or] one of those supernatural beings whom it was popularly supposed [David] was entitled to see" (P. 12). But in fact the narrator applies these words to Miss Trotwood. Betsey's unwillingness to compromise with reality in the shape of a male child provides the immediate link to the old lady who wins the caul, as well as with Miss Murdstone. The latter manages with great frequency to force the reality she encounters into a Procrustean bed of her own desires.

Miss Trotwood makes a revealing remark while waiting for the birth of the child she so strongly believes will be a girl. Arguing with David's mother, Miss Trotwood says, "There must be no mistakes in life with *this* Betsey

Trotwood. There must be no trifling with *her* affections, poor dear. She must be well brought up, and well guarded from reposing any foolish confidences where they are not deserved" (P. 7). She refers to earlier sorrows in her own life at which the reader can only guess here. But in doing so, she resembles another one of the Dickensian witches, Miss Havisham. To be sure, Miss Trotwood will strike the reader as a benign version of that awful personality. In her desire to manipulate a new life after the pattern of her own, however, Miss Trotwood mimics the mistress of Satis House exactly.

Mr. Chillip seems as mild as the Misses Trotwood and Murdstone seem harsh. He thus establishes a counterpoint in the novel that overturns our normal expectations for the traditional role of men and women in Victorian society. Throughout *David Copperfield*, the women David encounters will prove in general to possess greater moral strength, emotional resilience, and sheer energy than the men—whether for good or for ill.

After he leaves for a fortnight so that his mother may marry Mr. Murdstone, David returns to a greatly changed home. His reaction to Mr. Murdstone—one man in *David Copperfield* who is not weak—reveals much of the boy's character:

> I gave [Mr. Murdstone] my hand. After a moment of suspense, I went and kissed my mother: she kissed me, patted me gently on the shoulder, and sat down again to her work. I could not look at her, I could not look at him, I knew quite well that he was looking at us both; and I turned to the window and looked out there at some shrubs that were drooping their heads in the cold.
>
> As soon as I could creep away, I crept upstairs. My old dear bedroom was changed, and I was to lie a long way off. I rambled downstairs to find anything that was like itself, so altered it all seemed; and roamed into the yard. I very soon started back from there, for the empty dog-kennel was filled up with a great dog—deep-mouthed and blackhaired like Him—and he was very angry at the sight of me, and sprang out to get at me (Pp. 42-3)

From "a more highly privileged little fellow than a monarch" (P. 18), David falls to the lowest state possible. He becomes a little Oedipal monarch dethroned. He must share his mother's attentions with a ferocious man with black whiskers. He feels the hopelessness of the struggle keenly; David hates Mr. Murdstone instantly, far more fiercely than Murdstone's merely grim temperament warrants. Certainly, the stepfather does not treat his new son kindly, but David's extremely negative reaction to the figure of Mr. Murdstone, even before the child can know the man, unmistakably signals David's Oedipal jealousy. In this context one may understand David's portrayal of the other men in his life as mild mannered to be Oedipal revenge. The gentle Mr. Chillip, for example, does not threaten David's position at the Rookery.

David must now "lie a long way off"; perhaps this indignity more than any other shows his fall from grace. His life has previously been one of almost pure fancy. The house has been called the "Rookery" even though there are no rooks. The dog kennel has had no dog. These attributes evoke for David the love his mother gives him before the arrival of Mr. Murdstone. Such love is impractical, dreamy, full of fancy and a softness directly opposed to the "firmness" that Mr. Murdstone espouses (P. 45). But David suffers later in guilt for this gentle, incestuous love. Such love has great emotional resilience; David's mother remarries, and David himself takes two wives. Neither David nor his mother can endure the single life for long. They must always be giving love and frequently experiencing guilt over it.

David beats a retreat from the Murdstone onslaught into an imaginative refuge of dreams (Pp. 59-60) just as he does when, sent off to school as a hopeless case, he arrives at Mr. Creakle's only to find that all the boys have gone on vacation. "I remember dreaming night after night, of being with my mother as she used to be" (P. 79). His refuge in dreams of his mother as the loving creature she was before her remarriage represents a retreat into himself. Ironically, David slips into solipsism to find relief from his loneliness in imaginary communion with his mother.

Two groups of figures loom large on David's psychic horizon during his childhood. On the one side, David relies on his mother and the rough but affectionate Peggotty for love of a particularly possessive kind. David never really recovers from Murdstone's arrival or from the subsequent loss of the exclusive attention of his mother and nurse. In fact, when David's mother dies, the event has a minimal effect on the boy. To be sure, he grieves sincerely for her, but in truth she had already died to him since everything that David loves her for has changed. Thus, David may frankly say to himself, "If ever child were stricken with sincere grief, I was. But I remember that this importance was a kind of satisfaction to me, when I walked in the playground that afternoon [after hearing of her death] while the boys were in school. . . . I felt distinguished, and looked more melancholy, and walked slower" (P. 124). He romanticizes the death of his mother because he has already felt bereavement. His present feeling seems more like the *memory* of pain, than pain itself.

The other group of figures consists of the Murdstones, brother and sister. They treat him firmly where his mother treats him tenderly; they administer discipline where his mother and Peggotty spoil him. Although he blames Mr. Murdstone's hard treatment, David would in fact dislike anyone who supplanted him in his mother's affections. David immediately draws his negative picture of Mr. Murdstone from his need to hate a rival, not from Murdstone's behavior. The two neatly fit each other's psychological expectations. Mr. Murdstone for his part no doubt expects to find in David a pampered child in need of firm discipline.

These two groups of characters form David's personality between them. He comes to associate love with his mother's softness, and cruelty with routine and discipline. David evokes love of this sort in the language of dreams and fancies, of the "undisciplined heart" (P. 813). Cruelty comes to be associated with grogginess, a waking sleep that kills thought and activity. The dreary Sundays over which the the Murdstones preside, and which stupefy David, typically evoke this grogginess, as do David's lessons under Miss Murdstone.

This dialectic in David's psychic life continues in London. As shabby as the Micawbers may appear to the reader, they signify to David a laxness that he now identifies with love. The Micawbers' relaxed attitude toward money and their easy camaraderie appeal to David greatly. He contrasts favorably their Gypsy life with the unremitting severity of work in the Murdstone warehouse. David himself does not keep a tight hold on his own money. He describes in detail how he squanders many a sixpence on cakes and sweetmeats, often going hungry by the end of the week. In short, David's early life in London reinforces the same emotional lessons he learns during his childhood in Blunderstone.

Anxiety about his aunt's intentions after David arrives in Dover surfaces as exhaustion from his long trek overtakes him. He says, "It might have been a dream, originating in the fancy which had occupied my mind so long, but I awoke with the impression that my aunt had come and bent over me, and had put my hand away from my face, and laid my head more comfortably, and had then stood looking at me" (P. 196). David expresses, in terms of a dream, the desire for his aunt to treat him just as his mother had. He connects the tenderness which he desires with the dreamy state of "fancy" that sustained his imaginative life at the Rookery when he lay alone in bed reading about "Roderick Random, Peregrine Pickle, Humphrey Clinker, Tom Jones, the Vicar of Wakefield, Don Quixote, Gil Blas, and Robinson Crusoe" (P. 55). His aunt does not disappoint him. Again, life rises to meet David's expectations. Miss Trotwood engulfs the boy with loving attention.

ii

Miss Trotwood bestows a new kind of affection on David in the second stage of his life, one that violates in part the emotional rules he has learned earlier. She treats David in a gruff way that he finds alarming at first, though he learns eventually that one may express oneself severely and still love. Her tidiness further contrasts with the Micawbers' affectionate sloppiness. But David has become keenly aware of the Micawbers' managerial deficiencies, and thus he is prepared to accept the new mode of behavior his aunt embodies.

Two groups of characters dominate David's youth, continuing with some changes the dialectic domination of his childhood. On the one hand, David's aunt, Agnes, Mr. Wickfield, Dr. Strong, and Mr. Dick give David the emotional nourishment that he requires. On the other hand, Uriah Heep and his mother provide an antiphonal accompaniment of enmity to the chorus of affection that emanates from the first group. The two groups signal a rearrangement in David's earlier psychic *dramatis personae*, but a rearrangement of similar emotional predilections.

At one end of David's emotional spectrum lies Mr. Dick:

> Mr. Dick and I soon became the best of friends, and very often, when his day's work was done, went out together to fly the great kite. Every day of his life he had a long sitting at the Memorial which never made the least progress, however hard he labored, for King Charles the First always strayed into it, sooner or later, and then it was thrown aside, and another one begun. . . .
>
> It was quite an affecting sight, I used to think, to see him with the kite when it was up to a great height in the air. . . . He never looked so serene as he did then. I used to fancy, as I sat by him of an evening, on a green slope, and saw him watch the kite high in the quiet air, that it lifted his mind out of his confusion, and bore it . . . into the skies. As he wound the string in, and it came lower and lower down out of the beautiful light, until it fluttered to the ground, and lay there like a dead thing, he seemed to wake gradually out of a dream. (P. 216)

We watch here not one dreamer but two. Mr. Dick stands at an extreme end of the continuum of emotional tenderness that David calls love. Mr. Dick, in his mental confusion, resembles a masculine version of David's mother or of Dora. Indeed, David himself makes the connection when he gives Dora copying to do from his manuscripts, imitating David and Traddles' solution for Mr. Dick's need to feel useful. Traddles gives Mr. Dick copying to do too and thoughtfully provides a table to which he may run if he senses King Charles's head intruding into his consciousness. A patronizing tone mars David's treatment of both characters, as it does his descriptions of his mother in her more foolish moments. The danger from Mr. Dick's form of tenderness lies in the chaotic mental life to which it gives rise and from which neither David's mother nor Dora escape. In Mr. Dick's case, the chaos resembles madness of a tame, polite sort. David's uneasiness over the people in his life who act in such a chaotic way stems from his realization that they have influenced his own mental organization, and not necessarily all for the good. These entropic tendencies war in his own mind with his strong drive toward achievement. He fears a self-betrayal. His patronizing tone thus covers the concern that he shares such weakness.

Both Mr. Wickfield and Dr. Strong appear to contrast sharply with Mr.

Dick in their professional success and certified acumen. But in fact, Mr. Wickfield displays a morbid tenderness over his long-dead wife that he transfers to Agnes, allowing the child to rule the man. Wickfield is certainly not mad, but his alcoholic morbidity aligns him in helplessness with Mr. Dick. Similarly, Dr. Strong's worldly myopia likens him to Mr. Dick. Mrs. Strong suffers greatly from Dr. Strong's emotional ineptitude, and David demonstrates his bias in the Doctor's favor when he continues to treat Mrs. Strong like something unclean despite her innocence. In his rejection of her, David attempts to protect vicariously the part of his soul that demands utter emotional loyalty from his own loved ones. Above all, he wishes to avoid repeating the agony of his early Oedipal loss even at secondhand. Thus, he defends Dr. Strong from a similar psychic danger—the loss of a loved one—out of a desire for self-protection. In spite of all his efforts to avoid such deprivation, however, David loses Dora in death. By then, the emotional picture has changed, though, so that the loss does not hurt as much as it otherwise would have. David has already prepared a replacement.

David's aunt and Agnes add the only new ingredients to David's mental stew in his youth. They combine to show David that love may take a different form than his mother's tenderheartedness and yet be love. The two treat David with a firmness that hitherto only the Murdstones have shown. Thus both Miss Trotwood and Agnes become vital to David's emotional development. Underneath their apparently disciplined love lies a more complicated set of impulses, however. Miss Trotwood hides a wayward lover from the world, concealing too a susceptibility to emotional blackmail that aligns her with David's mother. Similarly, Agnes participates knowingly in the destructive psychic game Mr. Wickfield plays. The idea of sacrifice appeals to her so much that she cheerfully gives her youth to her father and her womanhood to David without any reasonable expectation of return. Both Miss Trotwood and Agnes display a pliancy in matters of the heart that endears them to David but that warns the reader that the two women are not the models of self-discipline David wishes to think. Indeed, we may suspect that David tries to hoodwink us and perhaps himself as well here. These two women allow him the luxury of having his love both ways—at least apparently.

The other group of players in David's youthful psychodrama consists of Uriah and his mother. Like Quilp's superficial politeness, Uriah's servile flattery thinly conceals a ferocious desire to manipulate all the other characters he can. It is the villain's psychic greed on a grand scale. His mother merely seconds him in all that he does. He reveals himself to the reader in his annoying physical tics—hand rubbing and wriggling like an eel, as Miss Trotwood remarks—as well as in his villainous appearance. Uriah's desire to manipulate represents a variation on the Murdstone theme of firmness, and one that poses grave problems for David's psychic growth. David often declares his debt to Agnes and Miss Trotwood for teaching him discipline. But Uriah demonstrates to David the dangers of the extreme form of "firmness." Uriah's self-repression leads to the ritualistic hand rubbing, wriggling, and the like. He cannot help these obsessive gestures. When Miss Trotwood explodes in exasperation over Uriah's wriggling in chapter 39, Uriah does manage to restrain his compulsive activity, but only for a brief while. In chapter 52, when Uriah finds himself assailed on all sides, he utterly forgets all self-control, writhing and rubbing himself into a perfect fury. Uriah's example shows David that one risks (as Quilp did) losing all self-control in the practice of firmness, when firmness means manipulating others.

One may wonder why David troubles himself with this repugnant creature at all. David belongs to a higher social class, has different interests and passions, and rarely even meets Uriah socially. Why then should he find himself at once so powerfully attracted to and repelled by Uriah? Uriah almost always addresses only David when confronted by a room full of adversaries, as if David were the instigator of all Uriah's misfortunes. During Uriah's unmasking, for instance, he turns on David, saying, "You shall prove this, you Copperfield," despite Micawber's active role in Uriah's undoing (P. 753) and David's passive one. Further, Uriah often unctuously attests to his special fondness for David. Even after their most alarming confrontation, when David slaps Uriah for slandering Mrs. Strong, Uriah insists on forgiving David for the blow. David revealingly remarks, "He knew me better than I knew myself" (P. 621). For once, David is right: Uriah understands quickly, for example, that David loves Agnes without consciously realizing it. Plainly, Uriah's interest in David is profound; he sees that they are rivals early in their relationship, just as their biblical forerunners were.

Two brief but important moments further serve to connect hero and villain. Uriah forces David to become an accomplice in the former's wooing of Agnes, well knowing how much it torments David. David responds exactly as Uriah wishes:

> I believe I had a delirious idea of seizing the red-hot poker out of the fire, and running him through with it. . . . But the image of Agnes, outraged by so much as a thought of this red-haired animal's, remained in my mind . . . , and made me giddy. He seemed to swell and grow before my eyes; the room seemed full of the echoes of his voice; and the strange feeling (to which, perhaps, no one is quite a stranger) that all this had occurred before, at some indefinite time, and that I knew what he was going to say next, took possession of me. (P. 381)

David's other experience of déjà vu occurs in Uriah's office when Mr.

Micawber twits David about his secret love: "'If you had not assured us, my dear Copperfield, . . . that D. was your favorite letter,' said Mr. Micawber, 'I should have unquestionably supposed that A. had been so'" (P. 566). Micawber's comment gives rise to the feeling "of what we are saying and doing having been said and done before, in a remote time—of our having been surrounded, dim ages ago, by the same faces, objects, and circumstances—of our knowing perfectly what will be said next, as if we suddenly remembered it!" (P. 566). Copperfield further remarks that he "never had this mysterious impression more strongly in my life, than before he uttered those words" (P. 566). Both scenes further connect in the reader's mind Uriah and David as rivals for Agnes's hand. The first, with its phallic overtones ("Agnes [was] outraged by . . . this red-haired animal [which] seemed to swell and grow"), reveals David's unconscious sexual rivalry with Uriah. The second signals David's unwitting romantic attachment to Agnes. David reacts less violently (and sexually) here because Micawber causes the association, and he is not David's sexual competitor.

Even in comic moments Uriah and David respond to each other compulsively. When he witnesses the awful spectacle of Uriah in a nightcap, David resolves instantly never to wear one again. When David leaves the Heeps for a long walk, unable to bear Mrs. Heep's puffing of Uriah any longer, Uriah catches up and wrings a confession from David that he loves Dora, not Agnes. A relieved Uriah responds with, "I'm sure I'll take off mother directly, and only too 'appy" (P. 574). Uriah makes his mother a succubus of which only he can rid David. In his fear of competition from David, Uriah uses even his mother as a tool in the plot to nullify his rival. In the biblical version, Uriah was not so resourceful.

Their rivalry permits David safely to express his own ambivalence toward Agnes. Uriah becomes the narrator's double, and David displaces on the eyebrowless villain his sexually aggressive feelings for Agnes in a psychologically dishonest attempt to convince himself that he has only brotherly regard for his future wife. The sexual tension is palpable as Uriah is unmasked:

> When his eyes passed on to Agnes, and I saw the rage with which he felt his power over her slipping away, and the exhibition, in their disappointment, of the odious passions that had led him to aspire to one whose virtues he could never appreciate or care for, I was shocked by the mere thought of her having lived, an hour, within the sight of such a man.
>
> After some rubbing of the lower part of his face, and some looking at us with those bad eyes, over his grisly fingers, he made one more address to me, half whining, and half abusive. (P. 749)

David can maintain his self-righteous attitude because he has absolved himself to his own satisfaction from having any "odious passions" for

Agnes. He does not fool the reader, however. Uriah's conspicuous rubbing of "the lower part of his face" further charges the scene with ambiguous sexuality; the wording strikes one as an oddly vague locution for "jaw," suggesting that the lower part of Uriah's face corresponds to the nether parts of his anatomy in general. Indeed, there is something inescapably onanistic about Uriah's writhing and hand rubbing. Displacing on Uriah these feelings permits David to convince himself of his pure regard for Agnes, but for the post-Freudian reader, this tidy arrangement signals David's ambivalence toward women. A self-deceived narrator indeed!

When David takes several weeks' vacation in London after his graduation to choose a profession, he encounters his old schoolfellow Steerforth. The meeting reveals further David's ambivalence toward sexuality and women. That night, David's dreams inform the reader about Steerforth's importance. The narrator writes, "Among pillows enough for six, I soon fell asleep in a blissful condition, and dreamed of ancient Rome, Steerforth, and friendship, until the early morning coaches, rumbling out of the archway underneath, made me dream of thunder and the gods" (P. 289). Certainly, David dreams about "ancient Rome" because of the childhood association of his classical education with Steerforth, but Rome seems to me apposite in another way as well. Arrogant, manipulative, and licentious, Steerforth the sexual predator disturbs the narrator greatly, especially when his depredations extend to little Em'ly. Indeed, the *connection* of sexual aggression with assertiveness in general in Steerforth's nature poses problems for David. Knocked about from Murdstone pillar to Creakle post, David finds Steerforth's easy, self-assertive manner tremendously appealing. But when he discovers that Steerforth's aggression encompasses women, David recoils from the combination. Throughout most of his youth, David idolizes the older boy. Seeing his idol tarnished severely shakes David's sense of the order of things. Moreover, David himself has had an attachment to Em'ly, and so feels partly responsible for the loss sustained by Mr. Peggotty and by Ham. He believes that he shares in the guilt not only because he introduces Steerforth to the family circle at Yarmouth but also because the affair reveals to him the implications of his own feeling for Em'ly.

The period of David's youth marks his realization that the love offered by his mother is inadequate in several ways—in its passivity, and its lack of discipline and of responsibility. But David has not managed to find a model of masculine love that does not create as many difficulties as it solves, as his preoccupation with Uriah and Steerforth shows. The affection offered by David's aunt and Agnes only appears to resolve the tension in the novel between love and discipline because their superficial firmness masks a deeper "softness" very much like Mrs. Copperfield's. As an adult, David will narrate his final attempt at a solution to this difficult internal dialectic.

iii

David begins his adult life in dissipation with Steerforth. Self-indulgence represents a new phase of the continuing dialectic that the narrator explicitly calls the struggle between David's "Good and Bad Angels" (chapter 25). The good angel, Agnes, comes to David's rescue at the height of his folly: She encounters him at the play to which he has tipsily gone with Steerforth. She warns him about Steerforth too on the next, penitential day, but David cannot take the good advice, so smitten is he (before the Fall) with his idol.

In Steerforth's brilliant light, Traddles, who might otherwise have provided a model of sound balance between self-discipline and affection, makes a dim showing. To be sure, Traddles's extreme passivity both in business and at home precludes any serious consideration of him as a role model for David. Traddles attracts the same sort of condescending treatment from David as do Dora and his mother. But Traddles deserves better. In the long run he succeeds both in his business and at home—the two Victorian tests of success that became Freud's "love and work." David wants to enjoy the life of a Byronic hero and at the same time have a loving wife waiting for him at his cottage. Because Traddles acquires the latter without living the former, Copperfield patronizes him, and unjustly so: David cannot play both rake and dutiful husband either. He wishes above all to escape the primal dilemma of losing his love to a Murdstone. Thus, he finds himself drawn to Steerforth despite his sexual transgressions, because David senses that the rake has the strength of will to command the security for which Copperfield yearns.[8]

Most important to his adulthood, however, is David's new love for Dora. In several respects, his infatuation represents a huge step backward in his emotional life. David's description of his love at first sight reveals why.

> We turned into a room near at hand . . . , and I heard a voice say, "Mr. Copperfield, my daughter Dora, and my daughter Dora's confidential friend!" It was, no doubt, Mr. Spenlow's voice, but I didn't know it, and I didn't care whose it was. All was over in a moment. I had fulfilled my destiny. I was a captive and a slave. I loved Dora Spenlow to distraction!
>
> She was more than human to me. She was a Fairy, a Sylph, I don't know what she was—anything that no one ever saw, and everything that everybody ever wanted. I was swallowed up in an abyss of love in an instant. There was no pausing on the brink; no looking down, or looking back; I was gone, headlong, before I had sense to say a word to her. (P. 390)

We find very much of love here, and very little of Dora. David has fallen in love with the idea of being in love—so much so, in fact, that the narrator does not describe Dora herself until several more paragraphs of prose and an eternity of feeling have transpired. Moreover, the narrator's description of her would fit any heroine of a hundred romantic novels: "the captivating, girlish, bright-eyed, lovely Dora. What a form she had, what a face she had, what a graceful, variable, enchanting manner!" (P. 391). Such an imprecise depiction serves one important purpose. It permits the reader—it permits many readers—to fill the gaps left here by the narrator with the reader's own ideal of beauty, captivation, and girlishness.[9] Dora may become each reader's individual love object as we identify with David and his fervid quest for love.[10] It is possible to respond on two levels at once to a novel like *David Copperfield*. At one level, the reader maintains a critical detachment from the narrative, analyzing the merits of the fiction at hand relative to other fictions he has perused. The modern reader especially may even dismiss the tale of Dora and David as sentimental nonsense. At another level, the reader responds to the psychological demands that the story makes, almost willy-nilly, identifying with the hero through every turn of the plot. The second level, indeed, has a logical priority over the first, because one must first *have* an emotional reaction to *criticize* it.

The reader begins to wonder why David does not notice Dora's faults long before he marries her. David's love is of the blind variety, to be sure. But David's term for her, his "child-wife" (P. 643), suggests that he has a more compelling reason than mere romance to marry Dora and ignore her faults. As many other readers have noted, David marries an image of his mother. He recaptures his primal contentment, or tries to; he marries a woman who has just as much tenderness to bestow on him as his mother. Miss Trotwood calls his mother a "Baby," however, and David himself realizes that his aunt is right when she warns him that:

> "These are early days, Trot," she pursued, "and Rome was not built in a day, nor in a year. You have chosen freely for yourself;" a cloud passed over her face for a moment, I thought; "and you have chosen a very pretty and very affectionate creature. It will be your duty, and it will be your pleasure too— of course I know that; I am not delivering a lecture—to estimate her (as you chose her) by the qualities she has, and not by the qualities she may not have. The latter you must develop in her, if you can. And if you cannot, child," here my aunt rubbed her nose, "you must just accustom yourself to do without 'em. . . . This is marriage, Trot; and Heaven bless you both in it, for a pair of babes in the woods as you are!" (P. 639)

As Miss Trotwood can see quite clearly, David and Dora's marriage cannot work. David wishes to recapture his childhood contentment, but he is no longer the same child that he was in the Rookery. He demands more of his wife than mere affection, though he does not understand his desires until too late. He has bought security at a high emotional price. Ironically, he condemns himself to the very loneliness he wishes to avoid. Dora cannot share with him in his trials and triumphs, either at home or in his career.

So anxious is he to fall in love, and to fall in love with an image of his mother, that David hardly even looks at Dora before he loves her. To an extent, David creates his Baby, because he insists on treating her like one. He does not permit Dora to grow in the marriage. His putative efforts to cajole Dora into becoming a responsible woman do not carry conviction. He does wish consciously that Dora were more like his aunt or Agnes. But his unconscious desires demand from his wife a figure whom he may see as the image of his mother.

The news that he has suddenly become a relative pauper sends David once again to the world of dreams, where he "was hopelessly endeavoring to get a license to marry Dora, having nothing but one of Uriah Heep's gloves to offer in exchange, which the whole Commons rejected" (P. 505). The dream manages to suggest in a few words a good deal of David's unconscious thinking. The connection of Dora and Uriah Heep demonstrates the intimate joining of David's twin desires for marital and financial security. He wants his *secret* relationship with Dora made legal and public; he endeavors to get a license. But his currency, one of Uriah Heep's gloves, does not represent legal tender to the Commons. Uriah's gloves cover his *hands*, the hands that he constantly rubs in a masturbatory gesture: David offers sexual currency for Dora. The sexuality of the hands David disguises in gloves, but even the Commons manages to see through such a transparent prophylactic fiction. Uriah plays a financial role in David's life as well as a sexual one; David wishes for Uriah's manipulatory power over the money that has suddenly disappeared. Copperfield senses his status as a gentleman slipping away from him and considers for a moment adopting Uriah's methods to get the money and the status back. He softens Uriah's presence in the dream, however, by encasing those symbolically powerful hands in gloves. David does not consciously consider using Uriah's conniving ways, even if he knew precisely what they entailed, because he cannot square such aggressive behavior with the "good" passivity that comes ultimately from his mother.

David attempts to improve Dora's character by keeping her much in Agnes' company. Agnes herself counsels patience, as his aunt did. But David finds hope even in Agnes' muted response:

> I never heard such sweet forbearing kindness expressed in a voice, as she expressed in making [her] reply. It was as if I had seen her admiringly and tenderly embracing Dora, and tacitly reproving me, by her considerate protection, for my hot haste in fluttering that little heart. It was as if I had seen

> Dora in all her fascinating artlessness, caressing Agnes, and thanking her, and coaxingly appealing against me, and loving me with all her childish innocence. (Pp. 568–69)

David's sensual fantasy demonstrates clearly his desire that Agnes compensate for Dora's failings. In his fantasy, David has both women's love at the same time. David imagines a ménage à trois that at once mitigates the feeling of loss that the choice of Dora over Agnes induces and satisfies his unacknowledged sexual desire for Agnes. David's remaining Oedipal lust for Dora as an image of his mother further charges the scene with tension.

Agnes battles against Uriah for David's soul as his love for Dora wanes. On the surface, David's hostility toward Uriah would seem to preclude any serious risk of the hero going over to the devil's side. David is more vulnerable than he knows through his affection for Agnes, especially because he does not realize how much he loves her. Uriah enlists David despite himself in the former's wooing of Agnes, at the same time as David enlists Agnes in his wooing and correction of Dora. The parallel efforts underscore how similar David and Uriah are in their attempts to win security for themselves. The narrator continues the parallel between David and Uriah by juxtaposing David's growing realization of Dora's limits with Uriah's unmasking of Mrs. Strong's apparent perfidy. For both men, it is possession of more than simply the linguistic kind! Both take the role of realistic spoiler, in effect, in a would-be romantic world. The seeming fragility of the relationship between Dr. Strong and his wife pointedly suggests to David that marital realism may destroy his own romance as well. He must correct Dora with great care or—better yet—not at all.

David expresses his growing understanding of the problems in his relationship with Dora even before their union in a dream image: "I occasionally wished I could venture a hint to Miss Lavinia, that she treated the darling of my heart a little too much like a plaything; and I sometimes awoke, as it were, wondering to find that I had fallen into the general fault, and treated her like a plaything too—but not often" (P. 605). David means that he does not often awake, rather immersing himself in a dream that cannot last, that he already knows he must awaken from to face the ambiguous and harsher light of reality.

David's efforts to remedy his marital situation at first appear to have worth; he tries to instill in Dora business sense, to teach her to keep an account book, and the like. In the process, David seems to acquire the "firmness" he has lacked throughout the novel. Dora's inability to grasp the commercial aspects of life is so complete, however, that David finds it all too easy to play the firm husband. He has not really solved the conflict within himself between his desires for all-encompassing love such as his mother once gave him and for the self-control that might enable him to prevent losing such love again. David's attempts to achieve a final peace between the warring parts of his personality fill the narrative until its very end.

The melodramatic story of Em'ly and Steerforth supplies an illustrative counterpoint to David's own history.[11] In his ruthless exploitation of Em'ly's sexuality, Steerforth shows that at its root "firmness" consists of absolute selfishness. The price of such firmness for Steerforth is self-hatred. Similarly, Steerforth's frustrated lover, Rosa Dartle, becomes the victim of her conflicting desires. Her enormous self-control enables her almost to master her self-indulgent love for Steerforth. But she cannot completely extinguish her feeling, and she comes to detest that part of her that will not forget him. The narrator paints here an early Dickensian picture of a self-tormentor. Others in the gallery will include Tattycoram, Mrs. Clennam, and Miss Wade from *Little Dorrit*. What David learns from the self-tormentors whom he knows is not clear; it seems easy to reject firmness such as Steerforth or Rosa possess. These characters seem ultimately to help justify David's own behavior to himself. In avoiding extremes, he also avoids a genuine self-analysis here.

Uriah also torments himself. As David somewhat piously intones, "It may be profitable . . . to reflect, in future, that there never were greed and cunning in the world yet, that did not do too much, and overreach themselves. It is certain as death" (P. 760). The narrator's picture of Heep's evil nature is more realistic in one sense than Dickens's analysis of evil in *The Old Curiosity Shop*. Uriah has a socioeconomic background that helps us understand the forces that drive him to evildoing in the first place. As a corrective for the superior tone that David adopts, Uriah sneers in response, "Or as certain as they used to teach at school (the same school where I picked up so much 'umbleness), from nine o'clock to eleven, that labour was a curse; and from eleven o'clock to one, that it was a blessing and a cheerfulness, and a dignity. . . . You preach about as consistent as they did" (P. 760). In *David Copperfield*, Uriah schemes to compensate for all that he lacks, socially speaking. Even if he were to succeed in his machinations, then, he would not be content, for he would always have to struggle to keep what others simply are given. Like Quilp, Uriah must torment himself with the knowledge that all his self-control, all his ability, cannot complete what is forever incomplete in his nature. Evil in this novel, as in *The Old Curiosity Shop*, is finally a null set.

But evil is not always gloomy in *David Copperfield*. Uriah schemes compulsively because he delights in showing the upper class that it is not as superior as it thinks. Uriah's obsessive nature drives him to discover the hidden designs of all his acquaintances, whether he has immediate use for the information or not. This trait likens him again to Quilp, who also finds himself unable to resist committing a little wickedness for the sheer evil joy of it.

In the final pages of the story, David searches for a resolution to his internal dialectic. In the great storm on the Yarmouth coast, both Steerforth's aggression and Ham's passivity are consumed. The reader wonders if in the exhausted peace that follows some middle ground will appear. The novel tests its hold on us when it proposes just such a solution for David, who is recovering from Dora's death. David has retreated to his world of dreams again as he wanders across Europe, unable to resolve his grief and guilt. All at once, descending a Swiss hillside, David finds mental health again, in an epiphany that shows him letting go of Dora at last.

> In the quiet air, there was a sound of distant singing—shepherd voices; but, as one bright evening cloud floated midway along the mountains's side, I could almost have believed it came from there, and was not earthly music. All at once, in this serenity, great Nature spoke to me; and soothed me to lay down my weary head upon the grass, and weep as I had not wept yet, since Dora died! (P. 815)

It is what the modern psychologists call a "peak experience," a sudden cathartic release of emotions that have tormented David because he did not understand their root cause. It has a Wordsworthian feel and seems slightly bookish and unconvincing. Perhaps that is because not until later still, after his return to England in the bleakest part of winter, does David acknowledge his love for Agnes. The winter clearly points toward an inevitable spring that will follow. Significantly, David first visits Traddles, who has finally achieved the object of *his* desire, his faithful Sophy.

Here we must ask if David has truly found a synthesis for his internal dialectic. Has he in fact managed to temper tenderheartedness with self-restraint in his own nature? The book ends with a chapter entitled "A Last Retrospect." The retrospective chapters show us those periods of David's life in which he most completely lives in a dreamworld of his own making. David's school days, his marriage, and Dora's death make up the other retrospects. The book derives its motivation from the need David has to express and then heal the division in his soul.[12] At the end of the narrative, David replaces his old dreams with a new one. He writes, "Oh, Agnes, oh my soul, so may thy face be by me when I close my life indeed; so may I, when realities are melting from me like the shadows which I now dismiss, still find thee near me, pointing upward!" (P. 877). The narrator's archaeology in the end suggests a teleology, a self-myth of success and personal meaning established by dint of self-application and Agnes's love, and perhaps a Christian heaven beyond. As David puts it when he loses his money and must establish a place in life on his own, "Whatever I have tried to do in my life, I have tried with all my heart to do well; . . . whatever I have devoted myself to, I have devoted myself to completely; . . . in great aims and in small, I have always been thoroughly in earnest" (P. 606). The romantic aspect of this belief argues for a world view with coherence and order, but one that seems to depend on the narrator's successes for ratification.

Such a world view has great attraction for the reader; the book seduces us, tempting us to believe that our own efforts to find meaning and control will also triumph in the end. As we enter into the complexities of David's psychodrama, we identify with David's on-again, off-again archaeological search for self-discovery. We read the book under contract to see events from David's perspective. We take on his psyche, provisionally, while we read, merging our experiences with the text to arrive at an understanding that encompasses both the story and our own inner voices. The danger comes when the narrator resolves his dialectic with Agnes's love; the reader may feel cheated, believing that David has replaced his childish dreams with a more mature, but still fundamentally flawed and romantic dream of love.

The book seduces us too because it speaks to our own desires, fulfilling our naïve wish to believe that sheer perseverance can solve our own dilemmas just as it has apparently solved David's. The gospel of hard work sounds like a belief in a commonsense world where one makes one's own opportunities and where fate does not play capriciously with one's plans. We can see, however, that David's apparently realistic battle with the world is in fact romantically doomed to success from the start; fame and Agnes's love are already his under the terms of the struggle, and David's rival cannot prevail.

When we last see Uriah, he has become a comical hypocrite, able only to impose on Mr. Creakle, who of all characters deserves it. Even Uriah's comical presence disturbs, however, the reader's comfortable identification with David in which both narrator and reader find satisfaction. Once again, as in *The Old Curiosity Shop*, evil has been temporarily banished, but the narrator must restrict his vision sharply in order not to see the dark shadow of Uriah lurking at the edges of the well-lit hearth over which Agnes presides.[13]

Just as Uriah disturbs the peace at the end of the novel, so does the reader. We must relinquish at last the story that we have created in complicity with the narrator. Here the tale does not deceive us, for as it ends it prepares us to return to our own private worlds, neither necessarily truer nor more askew than that of the novel.[14] The very process of merging temporarily with another perspective teaches us that our individual holds on what we like to think of as reality are in fact fictions too. We stand to learn much from engaging David's dialectical battle; David's experience warns us vividly about the dangers of self-deception in wish fulfillment. Thus we may discover something of the way that we create our own understandings of that last, elusive fiction, our world itself.

4

In the Prison House of Fancy

In the wild wood they found an open glade,
around a smooth stone house—the hall of
    Kirke—
and wolves and mountain lions lay there, mild
in her soft spell, fed on her drug of evil.
None would attack—oh, it was strange, I tell
    you—
but switching their long tails they faced our men
like hounds, who look up when their master comes
with tidbits for them—as he will—from
    table.
Humbly those wolves and lions with mighty paws
fawned on our men—who met their yellow eyes
and feared them.
               In the entrance way they stayed
to listen there: inside her quiet house
they heard the goddess Kirke.
                    Low she sang
in her beguiling voice, while on her loom
she wove ambrosial fabric sheer and bright,
by that craft known to the goddesses of heaven.
             Homer, *Odyssey* 10.208–23

Little Dorrit presents a claustrophobic view of the world as a jumble of solipsistic prisons, a view that motivates the reader to discover what prison he may have locked himself into and to set about searching for escape.[1] But there may be none: "Far aslant across the city, over its jumbled roofs, and through the open tracery of its church towers, struck the long bright rays [of the sun], bars of the prison of this lower world."[2] The quotation suggests that freedom from self-imprisonment may not bring release in the world at large. The very phrase, "this lower world," tantalizes, however,

Mr. Micawber
David Copperfield

because it hints at some higher world to which we may aspire. Reading *Little Dorrit* sets a task for the reader. The claustrophobia in the novel induces the reader to search for a solution to the dilemma the book delineates: the "lower world" chains itself in indurate spiritual bonds while at the same time pointing to a chance for freedom beyond.

i

Book 1 of *Little Dorrit* begins with a series of contrasts out of which the theme of imprisonment will emerge:

> Thirty years ago, Marseilles lay burning in the sun, one day.
>
> A blazing sun upon a fierce August day was no greater rarity in southern France then, than at any other time, before or since. Everything in Marseilles, and about Marseilles, had stared at the fervid sky, and been stared at in return, until a staring habit had become universal there. Strangers were stared out of countenance by staring white houses, staring white walls, staring white streets, staring tracts of arid road, staring hills from which verdure was burnt away. The only things to be seen not fixedly staring and glaring were the vines drooping under their load of grapes. These did occasionally wink a little, as the hot air barely moved their faint leaves.
>
> There was no wind to make a ripple on the foul water within the harbour, or on the beautiful sea without. The line of demarcation between the two colours, black and blue, showed the point which the pure would not pass; but it lay as quiet as the abominable pool, with which it never mixed. (P. 1)[3]

We have entered a prison house of fiction; our activities are circumscribed by the text. The narrator forces our attention on a curiously passive scene, a city prostrated by the "burning" sun. The prose itself catches the reader's interest, first by the very absence of active verbs, and then by the repetition of certain words. The city has developed a "staring habit." The text repeats "staring" until the reader may find himself "stared out of countenance" by the story, much as the stranger does by the city. "Staring" loses its meaning for the reader and becomes an obstacle to understanding. The repetition of "white" has much the same effect. The self-conscious prose creates interest in a passive scene; the self-reflexive motion of the text matches the self-absorption of the city, which regards itself with an unblinking stare. Thus the narrator creates literary fruit out of an unfruitful cityscape, a characteristic gesture of literary realism. He will repeat the gesture inside the prison at Marseilles.

The third paragraph contrasts the "abominable pool" of the harbor with the "beautiful sea" beyond, beginning a contrast between inside and outside that is central to the theme of the prison. We wonder what has created such an absolute demarcation. The text tells us: "Hindoos, Russians, Chinese, Spaniards, Portuguese, Englishmen, Frenchmen, Genoese, Neapolitans, Venetians, Greeks, Turks, descendants from all the builders of Babel, come to trade at Marseilles, sought the shade alike" (P. 1). Here is a multitude of nationalities gathered together for one purpose—trade. Or rather two purposes: the staring sun introduces in all a desire for escape, a desire that readers perhaps share, because they too have been stared out of countenance. But this mass of humanity does not provide the story which we readers crave. Our eyes blur at the prodigious list, and we have not yet found a tale. Indeed, the text only recreates the Tower of Babel, an ironic gesture that asks us to view humanity as a whole like the fair and foul landscape. The text enters now the realm of satire, a realm with purposes contrary to those of the opening sentence. History details the differences, and satire the similarities, among peoples.

In sharp contrast to the passive opening paragraphs, the description of the prison teems with active "vermin." The prose switches from an ironic to a moral mode:

> In Marseilles that day there was a villainous prison. In one of its chambers, so repulsive a place that even the obstrusive stare blinked at it, and left it to such refuse of reflected light as it could find for itself, were two men. Besides the two men, a notched and disfigured bench, immovable from the wall, with a draught-board rudely hacked upon it with a knife, a set of draughts, made of old buttons and soup bones, a set of dominoes, two mats, and two or three wine bottles. That was all the chamber held, exclusive of rats and other unseen vermin, in addition to the seen vermin, the two men.
>
> It received such light as it got, through a grating of iron bars, fashioned like a pretty large window, by means of which it could always be inspected from the gloomy staircase on which the grating gave. (P. 2)

The sun does not reach inside the prison; the narrator signals its moral obscurity with its visual obscurity at the same time as he contrasts the glaring light outside the prison with the gloom inside. Again, the description lacks strong verbs, or verbs at all—the third sentence has none. The dim light reveals the refuse of society. Claustrophobic and unclean, the cell houses society's unwanted. The world pays a price to have its way, however: It must watch these vermin constantly. This irony centers on the "large window" through which the vermin are watched by the polite society that does not want to see them. A lynch mob waits outside, prevented at the moment from carrying out its aggressive impulses. The lack of verbs underscores this fervid inactivity, so expressive of the imprisoned state.

The draughtboard shares in the purposeful purposelessness that typifies the cell and its inmates. Confined to an institution that takes all power of decision away from them, the prisoners mirror the roles we take on in games. We forego the normal responsibilities of life, submitting to the special rules and hardships a game imposes. Similarly, the prisoners find release from responsibility, even a freedom, in their very incarceration.

The qualified "freedom" that Blandois and John Baptist have gives rise to a prisoner's hierarchy. Blandois insists on being treated like a "gentleman" (P. 9). He receives deferential treatment from the jailer, who procures more agreeable food for him. Blandois marks himself as one of society's perpetual inmates by his compulsion to play the game of one-upmanship, the only one the institution lets him play. Cavalletto, on the other hand, prides himself on his adaptability. He says, "It's all one, master. . . . I can wake when I will, I can sleep when I will. It's all the same" (P. 5). Cavalletto's game preserves the illusion of freedom in adaptability. Exterior constraints have no terror for a man who remains malleable in the face of all exigencies. Cavalletto always knows the time and place; he preserves identity by adhering to his own internal schedule in a rigidly structured prison. The two men thus each wage a personal dialectical struggle with the prison, attempting to hold on to at least the illusion of autonomy in an institutional setting. In their attempts, they parallel the Dorrits' responses to prison life, as we shall see.

The jailer and his daughter's visit sharpens the moral picture that the reader has begun to form of these two vagabonds. The girl shrinks from Blandois, regarding him "with evident dread" (P. 7). Yet she finds John Baptist pitiable and hands him his bread with "ready confidence," passing her hand "caressingly over his face" (P. 7). Clearly, we may trust the latter with children; he is guilty, no doubt, of a crime forced on him by the cruel economics of his impoverished life. We get a more ominous picture, however, of Blandois. Like Browning's monologists, he begins to talk after the jailer leaves, and he will not stop talking until he has enabled us to complete our moral analysis of the man. We learn, obliquely, that Blandois has murdered his wife and may be guilty of other crimes as well. The narrator tells us, "[Blandois] stepped aside to the ledge where the vine-leaves yet lay strewn about, collected two or three and stood wiping his hands upon them, with his back to the light" (P. 12). The action reminds us of Pilate or of Lady Macbeth. This nineteenth-century villain apparently feels guilt at some level of his corrupt soul, which he signals to the reader with his obsessive gesture. The light too has a moral aspect for the reader. It has fallen only on Cavelletto, earlier, suggesting that Blandois is a creature of darkness, a devil. He shuns the light here, standing "with his back" to it.

As a character, Blandois is defined by the moral code he flouts, just as he is restricted by the prison from which he insists on his independence. In chapter 1, the Marseilles prison has already become a symbol of social restrictions, but one that draws its power from its inescapable physical presence.[4] It is at once symbol and fact. The novel pushes the reader into making moral judgments about the characters by such symbolic manipulation. The ethical decisions the reader must make center on the developing dialectic of external prison and personal integrity of which each character represents an aspect.

The last paragraph of chapter 1 further guides readers in their moral thinking:

> The wide stare stared itself out for one while; the sun went down in a red, green, golden glory; the stars came out in the heavens, and the fireflies mimicked them in the lower air, as men may feebly imitate the goodness of a better order of beings; the long dusty roads and the interminable plains were in repose—and so deep a hush was on the sea, that it scarcely whispered of the time when it shall give up its dead. (P. 14)

The double parallel suggested between the stars and fireflies, and the angels and humans, induces the reader to adopt a moral perspective on the story and its characters. The last sentence hints at a time of judgment in which virtue at last will have its reward and evil its punishment.

The first chapter of book 2, "Fellow Travellers," describes both a countryside and a people in ways that link it with book 1, chapter 1, and with the developing dialectic between imprisonment and personal expression.

> In the autumn of the year, Darkness and Night were creeping up to the highest ridges of the Alps.
>
> It was vintage time in the valleys on the Swiss side of the Pass of the Great Saint Bernard, and along the banks of the Lake of Geneva. The air there was charged with the scent of gathered grapes. Baskets, troughs, and tubs of grapes, stood in the dim village door-ways, stopped the steep and narrow village streets, and had been carrying all day along the roads and lanes. Grapes, spilt and crushed underfoot, lay about everywhere. The child carried in the sling by the laden peasant woman toiling home, was quieted with picked up grapes; the idiot sunning his big goitre under the eaves of the wooden chalet by the way to the waterfall, sat munching grapes; the breath of the cows and goats, was redolent of leaves and stalks of grapes; the company in every little cabaret were eating, drinking, talking grapes. A pity that no ripe touch of this generous abundance could be given to the thin, hard, stoney wine, which after all was made from the grapes! (P. 419)

Once again we find ourselves in the autumn of the year; the lack of change in the season hints at the lack of change in the characters we meet here, the Dorrits, despite their new riches. In utter contrast to Marseilles, however, Geneva bustles in the brisk mountain air as night comes. It is decked out in the rich colors of harvest, of the grape, and of the toiling peasant. The darkened Swiss hillsides teem with the industrious harvesters, whereas Marseilles lay flat and passive in the sun.[5]

The travelers lodged in the Convent of the Saint Bernard, like their frozen counterparts outside, reveal themselves in their gesturing. We recognize at once Mr. Dorrit's insecurity, his older children's heartlessness, and Gowan's "mocking inconsistency" (P. 429). We know them well before the narrator gives us their names at the end of the chapter. Thus we understand the central irony of the second half of the Dorrits' novelistic life as it begins. The Dorrits have not shed their prison habit, though they have left the Marshalsea for a foreign country. Like Blandois, Mr. Dorrit exerts himself to rise to the top of his new society, just as he did the Marshalsea. Amy, like Cavalletto, continues to play a more servile role. The others continue unchanged as well.

The first chapter of book 1 prepares us for ironic and symbolic meanings in the rest of the novel by delineating both the fact of a dirty prison in Marseilles and some of its moral implications. We better understand, then, the irony of book 2, chapter 1 in comparison with its counterpart in book 1. *Little Dorrit* teaches us how to understand itself as we read. It avoids the danger that irony faces of being read literally, a danger of which Defoe and Swift, for example, ran afoul. *Little Dorrit* provides its propaedeutic chapter in "Sun and Shadow" by pushing the reader into making moral judgments about narrative facts to assimilate the fiction.

Chapter 3 of book 1, in which Clennam arrives in England, also prepares the reader for what is to come and furthers the development of the dialectic between imprisonment and personal expression. The return home for Clennam involves two journeys, neither of which he makes easily. The first journey takes him from his father's world to his mother's, from one kind of authority to another. The second, even more difficult journey takes Arthur back into his childhood. As we watch this second journey we see Clennam's characteristic responses to "the prison of this lower world" (P. 741).

> It was a Sunday evening in London, gloomy, close and stale. . . . Melancholy streets in a penitential garb of soot, steeped the souls of the people who were condemned to look at them . . . in dire despondency. In every thoroughfare. . . some doleful bell was . . . tolling, as if the Plague were in the city and the deadcarts were going round. Everything was bolted and barred that could by possibility furnish relief to an overworked people . . . all [was] *taboo* with that enlightened strictness, that the ugly South Sea gods in the British Museum might have supposed themselves at home again. Nothing to see but streets, streets, streets. Nothing to breathe but streets, streets, streets. . . . Nothing for the spent toiler to do, but to compare the monotony of his seventh day with the monotony of his six days. . . .

> At such a happy time, so propitious to the interests of religion and moral-
> ity, Mr. Arthur Clennam . . . sat in the window of a coffee-house on Ludgate
> Hill. (P. 26–29)

The passage looks back to the first two chapters in Marseilles. The mention of the Plague links the English city with the French one and suggests
imprisonment for quarantine again. The gloomy Sunday results from an
attempt by the evangelical middle class to quarantine the working class
from the moral diseases with which an idle Sunday afternoon might infect
them.[6] The closing of houses of amusement mimics the "bolted and barred"
prison of Marseilles. Finally, the "spent toiler" in London suffers monotony
hardly less oppressive than that of the prisoner of Marseilles.

At the same time, too, the passage hints at Arthur's subsequent experience of London. Arthur is at once as foreign and as familiar in London as
the ugly South Sea gods. In China most of his life, he returns to English
customs that must seem (at first) very strange to him. Yet the rest of the
chapter makes clear that Arthur has never left England at all, at least the
England of his mother's authority.

The dreary Sunday on which he arrives reminds him of identical Sundays during his childhood. Now as then, Monotony rules, with Mrs. Clennam as its queen: "His mother, stern of face and unrelenting of heart, would
sit all day behind a Bible—bound like her own construction of it in the
hardest, barest, and straitest boards, with one dinted ornament on the cover
like the drag of a chain, and a wrathful sprinkling of red upon the edges
of the leaves" (P. 30). The paucity of ornament on the book mirrors the
dearth of "fancy" (P. 40) in the breast of Arthur's mother. The severe treatment has had its effect on the son: Here, Arthur's response to the closed
doors of London shows he cannot easily create his own amusement.

Arthur has not let his "fancy" die utterly, however. The word suggests
all that Arthur manages to keep for his own as a lad under his mother's
fearsome eye, as a young man under the yoke of business, and finally as a
lonely bachelor in isolation. The narrator makes the continuity explicit at
the end of the chapter:

> The airy folly of a boy's love had found its way even into the house, and he
> had been as wretched under its hopelessness as if the house had been a castle
> of romance. Little more than a week ago at Marseilles, the face of the pretty
> girl from whom he had parted with regret, had had an unusual interest for
> him, and tender hold upon him, because of some resemblance, real or imag-
> ined, *to this first face that had soared out of his gloomy life into the bright glo-*
> *ries of fancy.* He leaned upon the sill of the long, low window, and . . . began
> to dream. For, it had been the uniform tendency of this man's life . . . to make
> him a dreamer, after all. (P. 40, emphasis added)

Romantic love provides an escape for the young boy into his daydreams, where his mother cannot prevent the fulfillment of cherished fancies. Romantic love provides too an escape for the mature man from the tedium of the business world. Arthur reveals much when he admits that Pet Meagles reminds him of his first love, because he evidently draws on the coincidence for assurance that he does not hope vainly as he did when a boy. Like David's dreams in *David Copperfield*, Arthur's fancy tells him that life may be lived as though it were a fairy tale and he the youngest son destined to win the girl in the end.

In the fairy tale, the third son wins also because of his good nature, whereas the older sons are proud and mean. We do not have to probe Arthur's self-doubt too deeply to discover egotism, assurance that he can (passively) play the successful role of the third son. Arthur's shock of understanding near the end of the novel, when he learns that Little Dorrit loves him, is really a shock of *recognition* in this sense.

The narrator makes a further thematic connection in the third chapter. Responding to Mrs. Clennam's fierce construction of the Bible, he says, "As if it, of all books! were a fortification against sweetness of temper, natural affection, and gentle intercourse" (P. 30). Her grim reading connects with the "horrible tract which commenced business with the poor child by asking him in its title, why was he going to Perdition?—a piece of Curiosity that he really in a frock and drawers was not in a condition to satisfy" (P. 30). The narrator refers to "a parenthesis in every other line [of the tract] with some such hiccuping reference as 2 Ep. Thess. c. iii. v. 6 & 7" (P. 30). The passage referred to bears quotation, for though it comes from the New Testament, it sounds like the Old: "Now we command you, brethren, in the name of our Lord Jesus Christ, that ye withdraw yourselves from every brother that walketh disorderly, and not after the tradition which he received of us. For yourselves know how ye ought to follow us; for we behaved not ourselves disorderly among you" (King James Version). The counsel here to avoid transgressors does not sit comfortably with Christ's teachings, which command us to love our neighbors and not to cast the first stone. The reference derives, from part of the New Testament, a message contrary to the whole. In the same way, Mrs. Clennam derives from the entire Bible an unchristian message. Further, she has taken the passage literally, withdrawing from her "disorderly" fellow men by keeping to her room for fifteen years. Thus the narrator aligns Mrs. Clennam's authority, her discipline, a lack of imagination, and the world of work, with a literalist's "Old Testament" reading of the Bible. On the other side he aligns fancy, the son's resistance to authority, and the world of retirement and leisure with a "New Testament" reading for which the narrator implicitly argues. In the schematic view of reality that *Little*

Dorrit presents, "fancy" holds the privileged position over its opposite, imprisoning authority.

What Clennam finds on his return to London is a succession of failed relationships. Clennam can discover no hint of a thaw in his mother's frozen attitude toward the rest of the world. He cannot escape the trap of the past spent under her unloving eye. Every exchange between the two reawakens ghosts from the past:

> She and his father had been at variance from his earliest remembrance. To sit speechless himself in the midst of rigid silence, glancing in dread from the one averted face to the other, had been the peacefullest occupation of his childhood. She gave him one glassy kiss, and four stiff fingers muffled in worsted. . . . There was a fire in the grate, as there had been night and day for fifteen years. . . . There was a little mound of damped ashes on the top of the fire, and another little mound swept together under the grate, as there had been night and day for fifteen years. (P. 34)

Present and past mingle here to such an extent that the reader may have difficulty distinguishing one from the other. "All seasons are alike to me," says Mrs. Clennam, suggesting a similarity with Miss Havisham in *Great Expectations* (P. 34). She also teaches Arthur the first lesson about prisons he learns in London. Arthur witnesses the self-discipline and self-denial that give rise to, and the restrictions that result from, his mother's self-restricted life. It takes him longer, however, to comprehend the *attractions* of the restricted life. Indeed, only when he himself retreats to the Marshalsea does he begin truly to confront the deadly appeal of a monotonous security like Mrs. Clennam's.

The satirist usually derives one of three lessons from a city like London.[7] Either he ponders the vanity of human wishes or the democratic power of a city in which rich and poor are crammed together willy-nilly in a small space. Finally, the satirist may contemplate the lesson about change written on the constantly shifting face of the city. Mrs. Clennam attempts to deny each of these profound lessons, but especially the last; locked away in her room for fifteen years, she tries to avoid the reality of human transience. As such, she becomes an object of satire; her effort is doomed to failure. But Mrs. Clennam presents a dangerous example for Arthur in his own return to the past. He attempts to establish a new life for himself in London, out from under his mother's glassy thumb. In his mother's house, he risks despair. Faced with the grim lesson of his heritage, Arthur may decide that he too is doomed to a sterile life with no escape from the prison of the past.

But Arthur renounces the business that has brought his family so little joy, and the step seems at first a positive one. By rejecting the chance to transform the firm, however, Arthur in fact demonstrates his inability to triumph over the past. Instead, he manages both to reject the business and yet to keep its psychic burden by taking on a sense of guilt about an unnamed secret crime of the House. Thus he actually frees himself only from its daily running. He does not live in his mother's house, but he carries it about with him. Like some great neurotic turtle, Arthur uses his shell to protect himself both from life's dangers and its joys.

One may imagine the anger and helplessness a small boy would feel against such an indomitable authority. Therein lies the source for much of Arthur's guilt. Unable to express them, he would have no other outlet for his feelings than to direct them inward. Such anger would produce guilt soon enough.[8] Further, the only way out of this never-ending self-punishment would be to receive some acknowledgment from the authority that it had been in the wrong. If Arthur can prove the management to be at fault in one instance, he may be able to convince himself that it has been so about himself as well. Thus his desire to right some imaginary wrong done to Little Dorrit springs at once from his guilt and from his wish to be free of it.

Arthur carries his guilt into his professional life as well. It may seem that Arthur's partnership with Doyce represents a positive step, but in fact Arthur acquires him for the same reason that he acquires Little Dorrit. Both become *causes célèbres* for him. Doyce too has been wronged in the past by the authorities, and Clennam once more takes it on himself to right the wrong. Again, the effort strikes us as misguided. The Circumlocution Office seems no more likely to change than Mrs. Clennam or the past.[9] Arthur acquires his two causes because the relationships give him a continuing means of alleviating his enduring guilt. As Garrison Keillor is fond of saying, guilt is the gift that keeps on giving.

Arthur's treasured "fancy," which enables him to outlive the rigors of his childhood and the self-denial of his majority, has a decidedly dangerous set of rules. Indeed, his code of conduct is inherently self-destructive. In its extreme form, after all, self-repression becomes suicide. We may understand Arthur's reaction to his business losses, in fact, as the logical, suicidal outcome of his need for self-punishment. He withdraws from his social and business life, insisting that the worst possible construction be put on all his dealings. Arthur's self-rule threatens to destroy the "fancy" that his restraint was called up originally to protect.

At such moments, Arthur seems dangerously close to the solipsism about which the book has warned through several other characters. A complete, self-contained world of fancy, after all, is solipsistic. Further, the person who cuts himself loose from social moorings, floating away on the strong current of splendid isolation, risks losing his identity in the tide, because we define ourselves in part through others. Miss Wade provides a characteristic example.

When we first meet her, Miss Wade maintains her isolation even in quarantine. Thus she excites the curiosity of the other characters and of readers. We wonder what secret this mysterious woman hides. Appropriately enough she receives an entire chapter in which to tell us. Her secret proves to be a pitiful one, however. Miss Wade is simply paranoid. Yet her sorry inner life illustrates a central issue in the dialectic struggle between fancy and authority.

> I have the misfortune of not being a fool. From a very early age, I have detected what those about me thought they hid from me. If I could have been habitually imposed upon, instead of habitually discerning the truth, I might have lived as smoothly as most fools do. . . .
> One of [the girls with whom Miss Wade grows up] was my chosen friend. I loved that stupid mite in a passionate way that she could no more deserve, than I could remember without feeling ashamed of, though I was but a child. She had what they call an amiable temper. . . . She could distribute . . . pretty looks and smiles to every one among them. I believe there was not a soul in the place, except myself, who knew that she did it purposely to wound and gall me! (P. 644)

Miss Wade's misunderstanding of others derives from a faulty assumption with which she begins life. She has believed since she was young that she can perceive two levels of human activity. First, Miss Wade watches keenly the superficial doings of those around her. Next, like a paranoid Sigmund Freud, she attaches a contrary underlying meaning to those activities. In Miss Wade's fancy, every simple act takes on hostile significance. She suffers from an extreme form of a disease that infects other characters in the novel as well. In her solipsistic fashion, she assumes that everyone else feels the same way she does. When other characters respond to her with affection, Miss Wade's ire is aroused. She reasons that others must be experiencing the same inner torment she experiences, and that they merely mask that turmoil with superficial blandishments. In Miss Wade's eyes, everyone else acts dishonestly. Thus she attaches negative words like "hate," "deceive," and "condescend" to others' positive behavior. For Miss Wade, hatred becomes identified as "real affection." She uses the wrong words for the wrong actions. The linguistic barrier that she erects condemns her to a solipsistic hell. But she is not unique in her isolation.

Other characters in the novel suffer from the same disease. Mr. F's Aunt, who fixes her vast hostility on Mr. Clennam as a convenient object, gives forth startlingly violent remarks in his presence. "'I hate a fool!'" she says (P. 150), without any real basis for the remark except her own malevolence. Or, "'Drat him if he an't come back again!'" on another occasion (P. 517). Such hostility represents an ultimate, idiotic form of Miss Wade's angry isolation.

The solipsistic disease need not take only a hostile turn. Maggy, the retarded waif, lives without anger in her own limited world. Maggy has one personal song that she sings again and again; she remembers the time she spent in a hospital during the illness that deprived her of her wits.

> "Ten years old," said Maggy, nodding her head. "But what a nice hospital! So comfortable, wasn't it? Oh so nice it was. Such a Ev'nly place! . . .
>
> "Such beds there is there!" cried Maggy. "Such lemonades! Such oranges! Such d'licious broth and wine! Such Chicking! Oh, AIN'T it a delightful place to go and stop at!"
>
> "So Maggy stopped there as long as she could," said Dorrit. . . . "and at last, when she could stop there no longer, she came out." (P. 99)

For Maggy, the vision of order and peace that she retains from her stay in the hospital compensates for the violent, incomprehensible, chaotic world in which she must live. Merely recalling the episode brings a smile to her face. Maggy demonstrates a positive side of solipsism: her withdrawal into her memory protects her from a world that does not need her and that she never will understand.

Maggy is not alone in her efforts at self-protection. Our internal fictions or fancies defend us from the barrage of stimuli we receive daily. We could not possibly remember consciously all that comes our way. Our own fictions bridge the gap between the stimuli that we are able to process and the mass that we will never assimilate. Our fictions too enable us to make sense of a chaotic world. By them we live, discarding stimuli that our personal orientations make irrelevant to us and retaining that which we believe to be useful.

Each character's fancy has a characteristic "signature" by which we may evaluate the whole. For instance, Arthur's inner world has a fairy-tale aspect of primary importance. Clennam pursues Pet at first with (what for him is) determination only to retire modestly from the fray when he learns that Pet has already acquired her fairy-tale prince. He does so knowing that Henry Gowan will not make a storybook match for her. Clennam eliminates himself nonetheless, however, because the role of "rival" does not come into his personal myth.

Mrs. Clennam reveals her "Old Testament" judgment of those around her in the patriarchal phrasing she employs. She is called, but from within, and she has a nagging doubt that her self-appointed role does not receive the heavenly sanction to which she lays claim. Uncertainty strengthens her phrasing: She wishes verbally to ratify that which remains emotionally unsecured.

John Baptist Cavelletto signals his ready acceptance of life with his frequent use of the phrase, "altro, altro!" (P. 298). At the same time, the phrase demonstrates his helplessness in the strange countries his acquiescence takes him to. Cavalletto becomes a prisoner of language in Bleeding Heart Yard; Mrs. Plornish's memorably useless, "E hope you leg well soon," typifies attempts to communicate with him (P. 297). Thus his convertible phrase shows at once the strengths and weaknesses of his approach to life.

Like Clennam, the other characters in *Little Dorrit* must endeavor to preserve their fancies against often hostile authorities. Daniel Doyce struggles with the Circumlocution Office for official recognition of his fancy, the useful invention that the bureaucracy refuses to appreciate, it seems, solely because it makes sense. Mr. Meagles fights a losing campaign for social standing against the aristocratic authorities who alone may grant entry into their ranks. Edmund Sparkler and Mr. Merdle both attempt to best the social powers, the first by refusing to recognize when he has been beaten and the latter by hoodwinking society.[10] Henry Gowan struggles with the society among which he circulates in a similar way. Gowan also tries to hoodwink the fashionable world into bestowing on him the accolades it reserves for the gifted artist—or con man. But he is not willing to work for his fame, however, and society's punishment for such hubris is condign and cruel. He achieves only limited success, just enough to make him wish for more.

The other characters in *Little Dorrit* must also compromise with external conditions, and the compromise that each character makes tells us about his or her moral standing in the novel. For example, Mrs. Plornish reconciles herself to Bleeding Heart Yard with a fantasy that helps her escape the urban grime of London. The description of her solution reveals where the narrator stands in the dialectic struggles between personal fancy and societal authority.

> Mrs. Plornish's shop-parlour had been decorated under her own eye, and presented, on the side towards the shop, a little fiction in which Mrs. Plornish unspeakably rejoiced. This poetical heightening of the parlour consisted in the wall being painted to represent the exterior of a thatched cottage; the artist having introduced *(in as effective a manner as he found compatible with their highly disproportionate dimensions)*, the real door and window. . . . On the door (when it was shut), appeared the semblance of a brass-plate, presenting the inscription, Happy Cottage, T. and M. Plornish; the partnership expressing man and wife. No Poetry and no Art ever charmed the imagination more than the union of the two in this counterfeit cottage charmed Mrs. Plornish. . . . To Mrs. Plornish, it was . . . a most beautiful cottage, a most wonderful deception. . . . To come out into the shop after it was shut, and hear her father sing a song inside this cottage, was a perfect Pastoral to Mrs. Plornish, the Golden Age revived. (Pp. 556-57, emphasis added)

The humor at Mrs. Plornish's expense here remains controlled; the narrator does not patronize her too much. He emphasizes instead working within given limits to achieve an effect. The artist compromises with the space allotted to him to produce something that requires Mrs. Plornish's fancy to complete. Her imagination enables her to survive the harsh life of the Yard. She creates as much of a paradise as industrial London will permit her.

An implicit contrast develops between Miss Wade's destructive fancy at one extreme and Mrs. Plornish's positive one at the other. The reader must judge Clennam's own fancy within these extremes, deciding to what extent Clennam affects those around him for good or ill. His fancy leads him to focus his marital attentions on Pet Meagles first and then to decide that he has become too old for love after his failure to win her hand. His fancy has a precious quality; if he cannot have Pet, he will take no one. We see the cost of such selfishness in Little Dorrit's silent struggle to maintain her aplomb when Clennam ignores her so thoroughly. But Arthur does not bear full responsibility for his failure with Little Dorrit. Her own fancy helps determine her role in the protracted courtship.

Little Dorrit's odd tale of the Princess and the "poor little tiny woman" illustrates her imaginative life well (P. 284). The tale begins with the usual King and his beautiful daughter, the Princess. But then it takes a strange turn. Little Dorrit does not make herself the Princess, the obvious choice for a heroine. Instead, the interest centers on the poor little tiny woman. We might then expect a story of the "Cinderella" ilk, but Little Dorrit rejects again the usual form of the tale. The rest of the story emphasizes the unassuming, passive nature of the poor tiny little woman. Little Dorrit insists that the woman never gives "any body any trouble," during the rest of her life or after her death (P. 286). Little Dorrit seems constitutionally unable to assert herself; she lives a life of self-denial. She has become so shy during her years of selfless service to her father that she cannot even make herself the heroine of her own story told in private to an idiot. Little Dorrit remains a prisoner of her own emotional incapacity and of her father's overwhelming need for her devotion.[11]

William and Amy Dorrit form a bond that remains as strong as it does because both father and daughter need each other so much. Mr. Dorrit needs another human being to prop up his precarious self-importance, and Little Dorrit yearns to serve. The two respond to prison life in a way that reminds us of two earlier jailbirds, Blandois and Cavalletto. Blandois serves out his term demanding that he receive gentlemanly treatment; similarly Dorrit exerts himself to rise just to the top of the Marshalsea, and no further. William Dorrit suffers as Blandois does when his demands are not met in the imperfect environs of a prison. John Baptist and Little Dorrit also respond in parallel ways to prison life. Cavalletto prides himself on his adaptability. Little Dorrit too is the most flexible member of her family.[12] Both take little thought of their own bodily or psychic needs. Cavalletto, always agreeable, lets such matters take care of themselves; Amy abases herself to such a degree that she keeps the great passion of her life secret, as she ministers to the rest of her family, the little mother in a patriarchal society.

The prison represents fixity in a world of change. Thus characters who choose to imprison themselves must in part yearn for that unchanging routine. From years of confinement, Little Dorrit associates her father's love with imprisonment itself. She connects the routine of their life with her desire for their relationship to continue unchanged. The perpetual invalid clings to his symptom despite the pain it causes him, preferring pain to the uncertainty of change.[13] Thus we may understand Little Dorrit's fainting spell on the day of her release from the Marshalsea and Mr. Dorrit's collapse during Mrs. Merdle's dinner party. Indeed, Mr. Dorrit proves to be even more unfit for the world outside prison than Little Dorrit. The Marshalsea brought him a courtyard full of subjects. The world at large, however, is not so ready to pay homage.

We find reluctance to leave one's self-created prison in *Little Dorrit* at other levels of society as well. The creatures of the Circumlocution Office prefer bureaucratic bungling to real work. The pensioners at Hampton Court would rather complain about their limited quarters than leave idleness for activity. Clennam himself prefers the loneliness of bachelorhood to the risk of possible refusal from Pet Meagles.

The novel shows its readers the dangers inherent in these characters' refusal to change. Fancy comes into its own here; it works its greatest effects within prison. For example, we have seen that Clennam creates a private realm of fancy as a child that his domineering mother may not enter. The danger is that fancy may become an imprisoning force itself. Clennam makes himself into a middle-aged, sexless, lonely man. He meditates on the past, finding justification for his present attitude. Clennam blames his current unhappiness on childhood misery. In his mental odyssey to the past, however, he becomes sentimental about it.

Other characters make similar mental journeys. Miss Wade's explanation of her perverse state parallels Clennam's odyssey. Young John Chivery's monumental inscriptions comprise his nostalgic homage to the past. The Meagles' Cottage represents both their sentimental retreat to the country and their enshrinement of Pet's dead twin sister. In a comic sense, the Plornishes' short "journey" to their Happy Cottage at the end of a day mimics the Meagles' behavior but at a lower social level. Finally, Flora Finching spends much of her time ruminating nostalgically on Mr. F and "Arthur—cannot overcome it, seems so natural, Mr. Clennam far more proper" (P. 145).

Some of these self-indulgent, sentimental fancies we may justly condemn, as the narrative does implicitly in satirizing, for example, Flora Finching. But the narrator clearly approves of the Meagles' memorializing their dead daughter, if not of their spoiling the living one. Further, the narrator presents the Plornishes' self-indulgence as harmless at least, and perhaps even beneficial. Finally, the narrator sides with Clennam, endorsing his nostalgic fondness for the fancy that kept his imagination alive as a child. Thus the novel argues for the precedence of the past over the present and of sentiment over emotional growth.

Here the novel struggles with itself. *Little Dorrit* has as its central image the prison, and the novel reserves its most ferocious satire for those who imprison themselves. Yet in endorsing the nostalgia that many of the central characters evince, the novel makes impossible any escape from these prisons that have their origins in the past. *Little Dorrit* thus cannot wholeheartedly encourage change, which necessitates transcending remembered traumas. The novel looks too often backward into the past for an England and a childhood that can exist only in the entrapped memories of its unhappy characters. Here, we may side momentarily with George Eliot, who wrote about *Little Dorrit* that Dickens "scarcely ever passes from the humorous and external to the emotional and tragic, without becoming as transcendent in his unreality as he was a moment before in his artistic truthfulness."[14] It is precisely in this sentimentality and nostalgia that the narrator goes astray for modern readers as well as for Eliot.

In his need to return nostalgically to his youthful fancy, Clennam creates a concomitant need for the very authority from which his fancy protects him. Clennam visits his mother because he must. Only in her does he find the authority that lends urgency to his own self-assertion. Escape for Arthur thus has become almost impossible. He waits on his mother obsessively, searching fruitlessly for escape in the heart of the prison itself.

On a social level, the characters in the novel require the authority of the government even as it restricts them. They need the protection it offers against creatures like Blandois, who lead parasitical lives, darker versions of the mixed independence and dependence of fancy itself. The individual cannot exist in isolation. Humankind needs its prisons, it seems.

The prison itself implies, however, an argument for change. The very existence of the Marshalsea and Bleeding Heart Yard argues for someone to right their palpable wrongs. A tension arises, therefore, between the nostalgic treatment of the past and the social criticism in the novel. The Preface to *Little Dorrit* shows that this narrative uncertainty has its source in the narrator's own fancy:

> The smallest boy I ever conversed with, carrying the largest baby I ever saw, offered a supernaturally intelligent explanation of the locality [of the Marshalsea] in its old uses, and was very nearly correct. How this young Newton . . . came by his information, I don't know; he was a quarter of a

century too young to know anything about it of himself. I pointed to the
window of the room where Little Dorrit was born, and where her father
lived so long, and asked him what was the name of the lodger who tenant-
ed that apartment at present? He said, "Tom Pythick," I asked him who was
Tom Pythick? and he said, "Joe Pythick's uncle."

A little further on, I found the older and smaller wall, which used to
enclose the pent-up inner prison where nobody was put, except for ceremony. But, whosoever goes into Marshalsea Place, turning out of Angel
Court, leading to Bermondsey, will find his feet on the very paving stones
of the extinct Marshalsea jail; will see its narrow yards to the right and to
the left, very little altered, if at all, except the walls were lowered when the
place got free; will look upon the rooms in which the debtors lived; and
will stand among the crowding ghosts of many miserable years. (Pp. lix–lx)

The last paragraph reads like an incantation. The narrator also returns
because he must; he too is a prisoner of his fancy. In the narrator's prison
itself, however, incarceration never becomes terribly unpleasant. It has an
inner sanctum that never actually confines anybody. It is only used "for
ceremony." Further, the "young Newton" adds charm to the place; the inef-
ficiency of his circular answers reassures us that the narrator's Marshalsea
is not so formidable a prison after all. The unusual mixture in the preface
of humor and indignation has its counterpart in the novel; many readers
are troubled by the combination of satire and realism in *Little Dorrit*. When
G. B. Shaw wrote that "*Little Dorrit* is a more seditious book than *Das
Kapital*," he was focusing on the realism in the novel.[15] We can see, however, that the fancy ruling this novel at once delights in and detests its vision
of Victorian life. It is both (seditious) critic and celebrant. Indeed, the governing fancy must find its own dream at last in part detestable because a
once-vital fantasy becomes as unchanging as a prison in the process of writing a novel. A creation becomes mere product, and the artistic energy
involved wanes.

ii

We may now see that fancy imprisons itself because it structures the reality that it experiences.

They all gave place when the signing was done, and Little Dorrit and her
husband walked out of the church alone. They paused for a moment on the
steps of the portico, looking at the fresh perspective of the street in the
autumn morning sun's bright rays, and then went down.

Went down into a modest life of usefulness and happiness. Went down
to give a mother's care, in the fulness of time, to Fanny's neglected children

no less than to their own, and to leave that lady going into Society for ever and a day. Went down to give a tender nurse and friend to Tip for some years, who was never vexed by the great exactions he made of her, in return for the riches he might have given her if he had ever had them, and who lovingly closed his eyes upon the Marshalsea and all its blighted fruits. They went quietly down into the roaring streets, inseparable and blessed; and as they passed along in sunshine and in shade, the noisy and the eager, and the arrogant and the froward and the vain, fretted, and chafed, and made their usual uproar. (Pp. 801-2)

The passage is chiefly remarkable for all that it leaves out. Clennam has practically vanished from the text here; the prose reveals the omission in the faulty construction, "went down to give *a mother's care* . . . to Fanny's neglected children no less than *to their own*" (emphasis added). Again, "went down to give a tender *nurse and friend* to Tip . . . who was never vexed by the great exactions he made *of her*" (emphasis added). Clennam has been absorbed into Little Dorrit. His putative rebirth in prison can only succeed with her aid; Arthur languishes until she comes dressed in rags to visit him. Clennam never really escapes his mother's domination. Mrs. Clennam passes what remains of her hold on Arthur, her guilty past, to Little Dorrit. When Arthur emerges from the prison, it is as Little Dorrit's husband. She will at least treat him gently; his father suffered under Mrs. Clennam's more exacting rule. But Arthur merely exchanges his mother for Little Dorrit; he does not escape from their now combined influence. Little Dorrit is in control. She manages to get Arthur to burn the infamous codicil unread, so that he never learns the details of the past. It is a gesture of mastery and illusion on her part, and passive acceptance on his.[16]

The seasonal rhythms of the novel further indicate the absence of change at its end. Books 1 and 2 begin in the fall of the year. At the end of the novel, it is fall again, a familiar season in familiar surroundings. Little Dorrit and her invisible husband engage in activities, too, that suggest little growth in their lives. They tend Fanny's children and Tip's illness until his death. Nothing, then, has changed for the children of William Dorrit; Little Dorrit still tends to the wants of the other two; Arthur and Amy's future life together receives two words for an epitaph: "went down." The narrator expands these two words into three, unremarkably: "went quietly down." More than that we do not learn. The last sentence emphasizes, indeed, the futility of human striving and the unchanging nature of humankind, who can be summed up in a few words: "the noisy and the eager, and the arrogant and the froward and the vain."

Yet when Little Dorrit signs the third volume of the church register, the clerk remarks that she has had her birth recorded in the first volume, has lain her head on the second, and now has married in the third. The association with the three volumes of the Victorian novel and the inevitable happy ending in the third seems irresistible. Has Little Dorrit indeed escaped from her prison despite all the contrary evidence? What escape does *any* character find from this hell of imprisoned human intentions that is Victorian England? To what *telos*, if any, does the novel point?

One character has "escaped" before the novel begins. The reader's first sight of Maggy tells how:

> [Mr. Clennam and Little Dorrit] were come into the High Street, where the prison stood, when a voice cried, "Little mother, little mother!" Little Dorrit stopping and looking back, an excited figure of a strange kind bounced against them (still crying "little mother"), fell down, and scattered the contents of a large basket, filled with potatoes, in the mud.
>
> "Oh, Maggy," said Little Dorrit, "what a clumsy child you are!"
>
> Maggy was not hurt, but picked herself up immediately, and then began to pick up the potatoes. (P. 95)

Maggy remains indestructible, whatever the world does to her. For all her feeblemindedness, she possesses a resilience few can match, because she cannot hold a thought in her head long enough to worry about it. In some respects, hers is an enviable state. The mere mention of "hospitals" sends her into ecstasy, and Little Dorrit's mere presence suffices to calm Maggy's most intense momentary fears. But her life hardly constitutes a model to follow; even if we would willingly give up sentience for peace of mind, we usually cannot. Maggy's prison remains impregnable. She cannot get out, and we cannot get in to join her. Mr. F's Aunt's freedom has the same limitations. More serious attempts to escape must be found.

John Baptist Cavalletto perhaps can lay claim to a limited freedom. His ability to adapt to any circumstances certainly helps him preserve equanimity. Perhaps his approach to life holds the key to freedom from the prison of this lower world. When we first meet Cavalletto again after his long absence in the story, however, he has been run down in the traffic of London. The episode serves no purpose except to introduce him to Clennan and to remind the reader that Cavalletto courts constant danger. His devil-may-care nature continually gets him into predicaments from which he has no idea how to extricate himself. Further, those such as Cavalletto, possessed of a naïvely trusting disposition, rely on fortune alone to protect them from evil beings like Blandois. We must look elsewhere for an escape from our earthly hell.

The other character worth considering is Daniel Doyce, the character in whom fancy and business sense unite. Doyce himself struggles with his foes in the Circumlocution Office with ardor, until he gives up and flees abroad. His battle with the office teaches him that no victory can be won against such enemies. Perhaps, then, Doyle has discovered that the only possible escape lies in flight. But Arthur Clennam has left the country, perhaps in a similar effort, years before. Doyce's bid for freedom proves no more successful than Clennam's. Both men return, inevitably. They come back to their prisons, after a foreign holiday, finally no freer than before. Doyce's readiness to return to their struggle after Clennam gives way under the strain shows that Doyce has never really left his battle behind him.

We must look again at the last page of *Little Dorrit* for some reassurance that all hope of escape has not died. A bureaucratic society creates the prisons in which many of the characters in *Little Dorrit* languish, but such a system also creates the possibility of freedom. The narrator of *Little Dorrit* offers no solutions to the social problems with which it confronts its readers. The very impersonality of the society depicted in the novel, however, leaves room for individual solutions to the general problem. Theoretically, at least, the characters in *Little Dorrit*, because of their very insignificance, have the freedom to create for themselves oases of contentment amid the general malaise. Even in this more complex sense, though, Arthur and Amy still have created a stifling environment in which to live.

Fancy plays most freely amid restraint, whereas authority assumes that without it all is chaos to justify its attempt to impose order. Both Arthur and Little Dorrit call up dreams to fill the place left by the authorities that oppress them, dreams that cannot finally satisfy the reader. Fancy denies itself access to complete self-knowledge in its effort to create a safe haven. Clennam responds in such a manner after his financial losses. He locks himself in the Marshalsea in an orgy of self-punishment. He refuses to complete the journey toward self-knowledge that he had begun on his return to England. Dressed in rags, Little Dorrit finally rescues him—showing the reader that even she senses that Arthur has regressed. She must now regress herself to assume the custodial role she has assumed so often before with her father and family.

The book concludes, then, with two emotionally scarred characters who have achieved only a limited peace. The reader has watched earlier an escape from the prison house of this lower world that prefigures what Arthur and Amy will undergo. William and Frederick Dorrit's uneasy mutual dependence sometimes obscures their real affection, affection that shows most clearly at the end:

> It was a moonlight night; but, the moon rose late, being long past the full. When it was high in the peaceful firmament, it shone through half-closed lattice blinds into the solemn room where the stumblings and wanderings of a life had so lately ended. Two quiet figures were within the room; two figures, equally still and impassive, equally removed by an untraversable distance from the teeming earth and all that it contains, though soon to lie in it.

> One figure reposed upon the bed. The other, kneeling on the floor, drooped
> over it; the arms easily and peacefully resting on the coverlet; the face bowed
> down, so that the lips touched the hand over which with its last breath it had
> bent. The two brothers were before their Father; far beyond the twilight
> judgments of this world; high above its mists and obscurities. (P. 632)

Here and in several other passages, the text hints at a teleological release
from the earthly prison. The world of *Little Dorrit* remains hopelessly
muddled, whereas the promise of the other world is clear and absolute.
Trapped and confused by the lower world, the novel looks upward to freedom and understanding. It only defines this *telos,* however, in opposition
to the world at hand; it does not share with us a specific vision of the distant world to come.

At the end of reading *Little Dorrit*, we readers must retreat just as the
novel does from any apocalyptic vision. The novel leaves us within the small
oases that fancy has found for its subjects. Our putting down the novel has
something incomplete about it. Like Cavalletto in London, reduced to repeating "Altro, altro, altro," we ourselves remain limited in our ability to assimilate the fictive experience. Yet, like the "Merdle disease," our fictive
representations of the world infect everyone to the extent that we participate
in a community. We defend our individual experiences of the world with
the tenacity of the "paternal Gowan," who, given the post of "Commission-
er of nothing particular somewhere or other," died "at his post with his drawn
salary in his hand, nobly defending it to the last extremity" (P. 201).

What, then, can we claim to have accomplished in our re-creation? We
have compared our own fancied pictures of this world to a self-consciously limited version of an imagined reality, the novel. Thus our own fancies
have stretched themselves in the effort to understand the different world of
Clennam and Dorrit. We have fused our former selves, now irretrievable,
with the novel. There can be no returning to the past, but we may find that
our ability to construe our own fictive universes has grown in the effort we
have made to understand the prison house of fancy in *Little Dorrit.*

5

A Visionary Boy

Then you will coast Thrinakia, the island
where Helios' cattle graze, fine herds, and
        flocks
of goodly sheep. The herds and flocks are seven,
with fifty beasts in each.
                    No lambs are dropped,
or calves, and these fat cattle never die.
Immortal, too, their cowherds are—their
        shepherds—
Phaethousa and Lampetia, sweetly braided
nymphs that divine Neaira bore
to the overlord of high noon, Helios.
These nymphs their gentle mother bred and placed
upon Thrinakia, the distant land,
in care of flocks and cattle for their father.

Now give those kine a wide berth, keep your
        thoughts
intent upon your course for home,
and hard seafaring brings you all to Ithaka.
But if you raid the beeves, I see destruction
for ship and crew.

                    Homer, *Odyssey* 12.122–38

Like David in *David Copperfield*, Pip, in *Great Expectations*, admits a limited number of characters into his psychic life. For the most part, his consciousness as a small boy centers on the forge. The ghostly Miss Havisham rises out of a fairy tale that he has heard and forgotten. She seems more witch than human. Pip reacts to Pumblechook and the others in Mrs. Joe's circle only at rare intervals, when they directly affect his peace of mind. He knows Estella and Biddy imperfectly; women become a mystery for him

Dick Swiveller and The Marchioness
The Old Curiosity Shop

early in his life. We can see, then, that Pip knows few characters well as a child. Further, Pip does not widen his circle much after he goes to London. He confines himself largely to the Pockets' home, his rooms, Jaggers' office, and Wemmick's Walworthian castle. In his memoirs Pip chooses to focus on a restricted field. His decision structures our reading of *Great Expectations*.

When we take up a first-person narrative, we are largely at the mercy of a narrator who may either conceal or disclose information as he chooses. No omniscient figure tells us what all the characters are thinking. We see narrowly through the eyes of one person a partial view of an experiential world. The autobiographical narrative progresses, indeed, by alternately disclosing and keeping secret the narrator's memories. What Pip reveals to his readers and what he attempts to hide structure the experience of reading *Great Expectations*.[1]

i

From the beginning, Great Expectations is remarkable for all that it does not—or cannot—tell.

> My father's family name being Pirrip, and my christian name Philip, my infant tongue could make of both names nothing longer or more explicit than Pip. So I called myself Pip, and came to be called Pip.
>
> I give Pirrip as my father's family name, on the authority of his tombstone and my sister—Mrs. Joe Gargery, who married the blacksmith. As I never saw my father or my mother, and never saw any likeness of either of them. . . , my first fancies regarding what they were like, were unreasonably derived from their tombstones. The shape of the letters on my father's gave me an odd idea that he was a square, stout, dark man, with curly black hair. From the character and turn of the inscription, "Also Georgiana Wife of the Above," I drew a childish conclusion that my mother was freckled and sickly.[2]

Pip leaves his birth a mystery throughout the novel, after alluding to it here. Time and place never become more precise during Pip's childhood than "their days [Pip's parents'] were long before the days of photographs" and "ours was the marsh country" (P. 1). Even the delineation of London has less of the journalistic passion for detail that one finds in Dickens's earlier novels. Pip's London seems to consist of a small collection of close places: Pip's rooms, the coaching office, Jaggers' headquarters, Newgate Prison, Walworth, the Pockets' home, the Thames. In the first chapters, beyond an evocative description of the marsh country, the reader receives little orientation. What are the circumstances that make Pip an orphan? When precisely does the novel occur? What is the name of the village in which Pip lives? Although we gradually get a sense of the era in which the action unfolds, we never learn the answers to these other questions.

A narrative strategy that leaves such questions unanswered attracts our interest. What does the narrator seek to achieve with this elliptical method? Further, we ask what this literary technique tells us about the narrator himself. Our goal becomes illuminating the hidden parts of Pip's psyche, and the psyches of other characters about whom he remains reticent. Where Pip preserves a discreet silence, then, the reader scrutinizes the text with greater care, suspecting that something important *has not* been said.

Such a reader takes on a difficult task. *Great Expectations* teems with secrets. A narrator's control over his tale cannot be complete, however; Pip may reveal inadvertently the very truths about himself that he most wishes to keep hidden. Further, what Pip does not himself know consciously he may disclose unconsciously to the reader. The quality of Pip's psychic fabric shows itself most clearly where the fabric is torn.

The middle-aged narrator connects his "most vivid and broad impression of the identity of things" and developing sense of self ("that the small bundle of shivers growing afraid of it all and beginning to cry, was Pip") together with the irruption of the convict (P. 1). Magwitch surprises us, to be sure, but the narrator's coupling of the scene with his sense of the identity of things must seem highly unusual to readers. The narrator presents the incident not as the terrifying event that scarred his childhood but rather as an inevitable occurrence. It becomes for readers, even before they can fully analyze it, a fated, seminal scene.

But the narrator does not make these associations for us. He brings the moment itself to life in extraordinary detail, relishing the convict's wit and ferocity and dwelling on Pip's helplessness in the convict's hands. The first mystery of the novel, then, centers on the relationship of this initial scene to the rest of the narrator's story. The guilt that Pip acquires from stealing for the convict colors the rest of his life. He always manages to find something new about which to feel in the wrong.

Pip keeps his involvement with the convict a secret, and he is unexpectedly aided in this endeavor by the sudden appearance of a detachment of soldiers. The only guilt that Pip experiences here, as he carefully points out, comes from deceiving Joe, the ally of his battered youth:

> I do not recall that I felt any tenderness of conscience in reference to Mrs. Joe, when the fear of being found out was lifted off me. But I loved Joe— perhaps for no better reason in those early days than because the dear fellow let me love him—and, as to him, my inner self was not so easily composed. It was much upon my mind (particularly when I first saw him looking about for his file) that I ought to tell Joe the whole truth. Yet I did not, and for the reason that I mistrusted that if I did, he would think me worse than I was. The fear of losing Joe's confidence . . . tied up my tongue. (P. 37)

Pip's analysis of this secret guilt rings true; his childish feelings of insignificance lead to fear of the truth. His animosity toward Mrs. Joe, which comes from her harsh treatment of him, precludes feeling any pangs of conscience about her.

Pip's response to his first moral dilemma foreshadows his return from that house of mystery and secrets, Satis House. Once again, Pip feels compelled to lie about his visit, and, once again, his scruples center on the deception of Joe. Pip links Mr. Pumblechook, Mrs. Joe, and the others in their circle together as cruel adults, and, in both instances, Pip wishes to get back at those adults who make his life miserable. His guilt derives from the wounding of Joe that must go along, it seems, with the justifiable deception of Mrs. Joe and the rest. Pip develops here a habit of prevarication toward adults in general; he thinks of Joe as an overgrown child. In this way, Pip learns at an early age the dangers and attractions of secrecy.

At Satis House, however, Pip finds the rules of the game changed. Miss Havisham does not fit into either of the two groups of authority figures that Pip has invented, because she seems neither obviously cruel nor obviously loving. In fact, she is indifferent to him except as a model on which Estella may practice. The first mystery here that Pip wishes to solve concerns Miss Havisham's attitude toward him. Why has this bizarre woman invited him up to play? Pip does not choose to believe that she has selected him at random. That would make him feel even more insignificant than he already does! As he discloses to us what transpires during his visits to Satis House, keeping what he sees secret from everyone but Joe, we realize that Pip's early experiences help to produce a secretive, self-contained man with a great need to believe in his own significance.

Satis House holds many secrets. Estella's inner nature, her connection with Miss Havisham, her true parentage, and myriad other things about her obsess Pip with the obsession of love. The fact of his growing love for Estella Pip discloses to the reader early in the novel, but he keeps his sexual feeling for her a profound secret. For example, when Pip fights the pale young gentleman in the garden and receives a kiss from Estella in reward for winning, the connection between the two events, the fight and the kiss, does not receive acknowledgment until much later. The reader learns from Estella near the end of the tale that she secretly watched the fight to reward the victor. The episode comes at the beginning of what might be called Pip's sexual career and controls it thereafter. Pip binds himself to Estella in all her coldness with that one youthful kiss.

Pip tends to reveal to the reader secrets that involve general insights into character and to conceal secrets that specifically affect the narrative. For instance, Pip indicates without understanding as a boy the relationship between Miss Havisham and her scabrous relatives. What brings Camilla and Sarah Pocket to the dismal old house habitually on Miss Havisham's birthday? Why does the old lady treat ironically Camilla's nocturnal pains? The greed of Miss Havisham's relatives and her delight in watching them endeavor to outdo each other in obsequious behavior toward her, Pip makes understandable to the reader without comprehending it himself as a boy. The origin of Pip's great expectations, on the other hand, the narrator keeps secret. Pip as narrator maintains a double consciousness well suited to his need both to conceal and to disclose to tell a good tale.

Satis House and its occupants only become more mysterious to Pip as he grows older. The secret of his great expectations seems to become clear in the gap which he hastens to fill between Jaggers' professional discretion and Pip's immature guesses. But Miss Havisham's lack of interest in Pip except as an object with which to torture Sarah Pocket during his farewell visit to Satis House suggests an unrevealed secret about the source of Pip's wealth. Pip remarks that he "was not expected" on his last visit (P. 148). He further notices, without discerning its full significance, Miss Havisham's "keen" "enjoyment of Sarah Pocket's jealous dismay," the "triumph in her weird eyes" (P. 149). Because he is so anxious to believe his fairy-godmother story, Pip does not realize that Miss Havisham's response would go beyond "triumph" over a discomfited relative had she, who watches over every detail of Estella's life, had a concomitant interest in Pip's.

The secretive Orlick further clouds the atmosphere at Satis House by turning up as a gatekeeper. Pip wonders about the apparently fortuitous connection between the attack on Mrs. Joe, Orlick's dismissal from the forge, and his subsequent position at Miss Havisham's. Pip's inability to think clearly about these connections points to a subterranean link of guilt between himself and Orlick, a link made visible by the murderer's use of Magwitch's leg iron in the attack. Moreover, we learn that Orlick hates Pip fiercely for their brief rivalry over Biddy.

For Pip, London is a city of secrets. The first one that confronts Pip on his arrival is a secret revealed: Pip learns that he will share rooms with the pale young gentleman himself, Herbert Pocket. By Pip's faulty reasoning, the link between the Pockets, Miss Havisham, and Pip's great expectations seems like further confirmation of the source of his good fortune. The second "secret" that confronts him Herbert Pocket reveals to Pip: the secret of how to behave at the table. A third secret: Pip himself extends the net of concealment to include Herbert's financial affairs. Pip aids him by establishing him in business without his knowledge.

Over the secret city of London, Jaggers exercises seemingly omnipotent control. The clients that cluster about him when he returns to "Little Britain" after a day in court testify to Jaggers' efficiency. (The name "Little Britain," indeed, both extends and restricts our sense of Jaggers' influence.) Each client and would-be client has an unshakable conviction that only Jaggers can save him. Wemmick, who possesses his own secret Walworthian life, adds to this uninformed opinion with expert testimony of his own, telling Pip tales of Jaggers' more famous triumphs.

For Pip, the most important mystery over which Jaggers exercises control remains the source of his great expectations. When Magwitch himself finally reveals the secret with a double handshake, Pip's astonishment testifies to Jaggers' ability to keep a secret. Indeed, the only time either Pip or Wemmick can say he has seen Jaggers at a loss occurs when Pip goes to him to attempt to force some information out of him about Estella. Pip does so by revealing to Jaggers secrets the lawyer himself does not possess. The lawyer's slight betrayal of surprise shows both the extent of his self-control and the force of the shock itself. The combination of Pip's emotional appeal and his revelations leads Jaggers to disclose what may be the first secret he has revealed, professionally speaking. He tells Pip—very obliquely—of Estella's parentage and Miss Havisham's role in the mystery. For Pip, of course, the episode has the further resonance of marking the one time that he is able to control Jaggers, who has otherwise so completely controlled him (and so many others).

If fictive autobiography proceeds by the disclosure of secrets, however, the example of *Great Expectations* shows the virtue of keeping secrets well. Indeed, a heading in chapter 51, under which Jaggers and Wemmick recover from the upsetting effects of disclosing so many secrets to Pip and to each other, reads, "The Virtue of Secrecy." Both Wemmick and Jaggers believe that they must keep most of their secrets to stay in business. In the case of Estella's secret heritage, Pip agrees. Presumably, suffering will be avoided if those who hold the secret of her parentage suppress it. In the same fashion, Pip conceals his involvement in Herbert's business to build Herbert's self-esteem. Pip discloses that secret when he realizes that neither his own ego nor Herbert's stands in need of such careful treatment any longer. After all, the two have well established themselves as partners together in a humble but successful firm.

Secrets concealed can trouble those not cognizant of them, however; Pip nearly suffers death at Orlick's hands because of his inability to understand Orlick. When the journeyman discloses his secret in the lurid air of the lime-kiln, the reader fully realizes, even if Pip does not, the importance of self-awareness in a morally ambiguous world. Self-awareness on Pip's part would have led to understanding the effect that his daily presence must have had on the underprivileged Orlick. But Pip largely ignores him, considering him a mere brute, until circumstances make indifference impossible.

As readers, we too must not remain passive, relying only on what we learn explicitly. We risk losing track of the narrative, becoming overwhelmed by a surprising turn of events. We must supply the analysis where the book does not, filling up Pip's silences with our own understanding. We need to develop alternate sources of information, clues that will help us solve the puzzles posed by the novel. We need a subtler language than the narrative one. *Great Expectations* provides exactly that in the language of hands in the novel.[3]

ii

Hands in *Great Expectations* signal a character's unspoken thoughts with great accuracy. A character's hands reveal his attempts to manipulate others. A character's hands demonstrate how effective that character is in controlling his own life. What a character says with his hands sometimes contradicts his verbal expression, revealing his unspoken or unconscious thoughts. The language of hands in *Great Expectations* is the language of power and control.[4]

At the opening of the novel, Pip likens himself to his five dead brothers, whose tiny graves suggest to him that "they had all been born on their backs with their hands in their trousers-pockets, and have never taken them out in this state of existence" (P. 1). The image conveys the helplessness of Pip's brothers, who gave up their lives so quickly, a helplessness that Pip shares. The convict abruptly ends Pip's moody reflections, laying violent hands on the boy, and turning him upside down in a gesture of complete dominance. The convict establishes control over Pip with his hands and his tale of the ferocious young man, "in comparison with which young man [Magwitch is] a Angel" (P. 3). Even as Magwitch manipulates Pip, however, the narrator shows that the convict's own hold on life is tenuous indeed. The narrator comments, "He looked . . . as if he were eluding the hands of the dead people, stretching up cautiously out of their graves, to get a twist on his ankle and pull him in" (P. 4). The image reveals to the reader how near death the convict himself has come.

The two rivals for Pip's affection as a boy demonstrate with their hands their actual relationships with him. Mrs. Joe prides herself on having brought up her small brother "by hand" (P. 6). She means, of course, that she bottle-fed him, but the expression takes on new meaning in Pip's narration. Mrs. Joe has brought Pip up with a very heavy hand indeed. Her hands are frequently in evidence, punishing Pip, doling out slabs of bread to him, dosing him with various medicines, bolstering his character with the Tickler, and generally brutalizing the sensitive boy. By way of contrast, Joe's hands never receive mention in the early part of the book. The omission seems remarkable because Joe is a blacksmith, a man who works with his hands. From Pip's point of view, though, Joe's hands are never there when needed, to protect him from Mrs. Joe's discipline. Joe provides an ineffectual leg when Tickler threatens, but does not give Pip the protection he wants. As Joe himself says much later in the narrative, "Lookee here, old chap, . . . I done what I could to keep you and Tickler in sunders, but my power were not always fully equal to my inclinations" (P. 44). Joe realizes that his love for the boy is too passive. Pip torments himself throughout the novel, trying not to condescend to Joe. But in fact Pip learns to look down on Joe's emotional powers long before he learns about more superficial class barriers. Thus Pip continues to treat Joe as a comic character after he has ostensibly made peace with him, begging Joe's forgiveness. Even as Joe cares for Pip tenderly throughout his illness, Pip mocks him for his verbal expression and for his attempts to write. Joe calls Camilla "Mrs. Camels" (P. 441), and his labors at the writing desk approach mock-epic proportions.

> Joe now sat down to his great work, first choosing a pen from the pen-tray as if it were a chest of large tools, and tucking up his sleeves as if he were going to wield a crowbar or sledge-hammer. It was necessary for Joe to hold on heavily to the table with his left elbow, and to get his right leg well out behind him, before he could begin, and when he did begin he made every downstroke so slowly that it might have been six feet long, while at every upstroke I could hear his pen spluttering extensively. (P. 440)

And so it goes. One remembers here Joe's effort with "J" and "O" early in the novel; not much has changed in the narrator's rendition of Joe, despite the claims of forgiveness. Joe provides comic relief here from Pip's illness and the drama of Magwitch's attempted escape. His role in the novel, then, remains a fundamentally comic one, even as he inevitably provides a tragic model of adult behavior for young Pip.

The most disastrous service that Joe renders Pip is not so much his failure to protect Pip's backside from Tickler and Mrs. Joe as it is the image of affectionate love that he gives Pip. Joe teaches Pip to undervalue such affection because it does not provide sufficient protection against life's hard knocks. Pip generalizes his understanding to create a definition of love in which human warmth has only a small role. This skewed idea of love enables him to put up with Estella's treatment as few men could. She combines power and coldness in the right proportions for Pip, who cannot much value what other people mean by "love" (tenderness) because it seems to him to connote powerlessness and pain. The dominance that Estella establishes over Pip, in fact, parallels closely Pip's later control of Joe. Both victims suffer greatly in their relationships.

As Pip first meets Estella at Satis House, the language of hands gives us accurate notice of who controls whom. Miss Havisham's hands are much in evidence, on her heart to demonstrate her desires, on Pip's shoulder to manipulate the young boy. But Pip's own hands become a source of intense discomfort for him when he begins to play cards with Estella:

> "He calls the knaves, Jacks, this boy!" said Estella with disdain, before our first game was out. "And what coarse hands he has! And what thick boots!"
>
> I had never thought of being ashamed of my hands before; but I began to consider them a very indifferent pair. Her contempt for me was so strong, that it became infectious, and I caught it. (P. 55)

Note that though Estella remarks on both Pip's hands and boots, the narrator comments only on the hands. Pip's hands become the focus for much of his self-loathing and others' disregard. Estella establishes control over Pip by means of her negative opinion. Similarly, Miss Havisham develops her powerful role in Pip's life as much with her low opinion of Pip, expressed through her manipulative hands, as by her class and wealth. Pip's own "coldness," as many critics have seen it, and his apparent snobbishness toward others may be traced to his early training under Joe, Mrs. Joe, and the denizens of Satis House.[5]

Pip first meets Mr. Jaggers at Satis House as a small boy, unaware that the lawyer will play a role in his later life. The description of Jaggers' hands, however, signals to the reader that Jaggers will be a character of great importance.

> He was a burly man of an exceedingly dark complexion, with an exceedingly large head and a corresponding large hand. He took my chin in his large hand and turned up my face to have a look at me by the light of the candle. . . .
>
> "How do you come here?"
>
> "Miss Havisham sent for me, sir," I explained.
>
> "Well, behave yourself. I have a pretty large experience of boys, and you're a bad set of fellows. Now mind!" said he, biting the side of his great forefinger as he frowned at me, "you behave yourself!"
>
> With these words he released me—which I was glad of, for his hand smelt of scented soap—and went his way downstairs. (P. 77)

Jaggers takes control of Pip without thinking, grasping the boy's face in his huge hand. Jaggers' characteristic gesture, in which he bites his forefinger to intimidate his clients, judges, and other lawyers, works well here both to introduce a character and to cow Pip. Like Pip, we cannot yet understand the reference to scented soap. As we come to know Jaggers in his office in Little Britain, however, we learn that the hand washing that produces the scent constitutes a ritualistic, Pilate-like gesture of cleansing that rids him morally of his clients. That he washes his hands compulsively further suggests, despite his denials, that he possesses a strong ethical sense which he must frequently appease.

Pip meets one other important character during his tenure as plaything at Satis House, Herbert Pocket, in a younger, more carbuncular phase. Herbert is all form and no content. His hands, vital to pugilism, appear only at the beginning of his humiliation as he claps them together to initiate the combat. His pretended expertise is a lie; he has no real strength any more than his relatives, the toady ones, have real affection for Miss Havisham. Similarly, Miss Havisham's Frankenstein-like experimentation on Estella has produced a woman who has no inner warmth, only a show of it. As Miss Havisham so memorably says, "I stole her heart away and put ice in its place" (P. 378). Pip himself catches the spirit of the place when he begins to tell fabulous lies about his experience at Satis House to his adult tormentors. A lie is, after all, the form of truth without the content. Herbert's name, Pocket, connects with Pip's five dead brothers, revealing at once his brotherly relationship with Pip, his initial ineffectuality, and his impotence as businessman and lover. Pip later revises his assessment of Herbert, but too late to change our vivid image of his helplessness and too late to change his name.

Pip's own potency seems to him confirmed when he learns of his great expectations. It is an opinion that Mr. Pumblechook apparently shares. He greets the transformed Pip with an effusive double handshake, a gesture that has great significance in the novel.

> "But do I," said Mr. Pumblechook, getting up again the moment after he had sat down, "see afore me, him as I ever sported with in his times of happy infancy? And may I—*may* I —?"
>
> This May I, meant might he shake hands? I consented, and he was fervent, and then sat down again. . . .
>
> "Yet I cannot," said Mr. Pumblechook, getting up again, "see afore me One—and likewise drink to One—without again expressing—May I—*may* I—?"
>
> I said he might, and he shook hands with me again, and emptied his glass and turned it upside down. (P. 145)

Only two other characters approach Pip with the double handshake, Magwitch and Joe. Magwitch shakes both of Pip's hands when he returns from Australia with the news that he has given Pip his expectations. Joe shakes Pip's hands in genuine affection when he visits Pip in his London digs. The affection quickly gives way to self-consciousness as the new difference in class between the two men becomes a barrier to communication. All three characters play the father to Pip. Pumblechook gives a hypocritical version of Joe's genuine affection. Magwitch attempts to give Pip fatherly affection too, but Pip cannot easily accept Magwitch's love.

Magwitch's handshake connects thematically with his grabbing of Pip in the graveyard. The convict's gestures evoke an enduring guilt in Pip that gives clues to his character. Pip, like Telemachus, searches for a father from the beginning of his story. He cannot say his father's name, "Pirrip," and so resorts to creating his own name. Thus, he invents his own identity and his own sense of the "identity of things." His identity from the very first is tainted with guilt. In the next paragraph, Pip relates to us his meeting with the convict. Pip derives from this experience a permanently guilty conscience that begins with the purloined pork pie and grows like an unkillable weed after that. His sister's hard upbringing and Estella's influence further nourish his guilt. Pip both identifies with the convict and suffers guilt over his first foray into juvenile crime. He identifies with Magwitch because, despite his terror, the boy senses that they are both victims. Because the convict consumes Mrs. Joe's food, indeed, both of them come in a sense under her fearsome authority.

From Joe, Pip acquires both an undervalued idea of the importance of affection in personal relationships and a feeling that he has let Joe down in failing to return what affection Joe does give him. We may also discover here the roots of Pip's so-called snobbishness. He never becomes comfortable in his role as fop. His uneasy vanity seems to me to reflect his guilt at having failed Joe, even as Pip enjoys as well as he can—the "harmonious blacksmith"—a gentleman's life in Victorian London.

From Pumblechook, finally, Pip learns the pretensions of a pompous adult who would always be taking credit for events over which he has no control. Pumblechook's absurd repetitions of the double handshake reveal how little he does have to do with Pip, especially as a benefactor. He would not have to try so hard if his contribution were real. Both of the other two characters, who have a genuine role in shaping Pip, use the double handshake only at key moments. When Pumblechook grasps both of Pip's hands, we may understand the claim he tries to make with that gesture, just as we understand the real and unstated claims that Joe and Magwitch make when they do the same.

By contrast with Pip's other benefactors, Miss Havisham takes on the role largely because Pip so desperately wants her to. He hopes to arrange things so that Estella will come to him by right, and Miss Havisham lets him think that may be possible.

> She stretched out her hand, and I went down on my knee and put it to my lips. I had not considered how I should take leave of her; it came naturally to me at the moment, to do this. She looked at Sarah Pocket with triumph in her weird eyes, and so I left my fairy godmother, with both her hands on her crutch stick, standing in the midst of the dimly lighted room beside the rotten bride-cake that was hidden in cobwebs. (P. 149)

The language of hands here suggests how passive her role is. Pip performs the genuflecting; he takes from *her* signs of interest. She stands silently, taking advantage of the overeager youth at her feet, both her hands idle on her crutch stick. By her very refusal to tell Pip the truth about their relationship, however, she exercises great power over him. Her ability to control Pip so completely demonstrates her astonishing genius in controlling others from her retired position. Like Jaggers, Miss Havisham has learned how to wield information as a weapon, withholding it until revelation serves her purposes. Her abilities match metaphorically those of the spiders who spin their webs amid the crumbling ruin of bride-cake. Miss Havisham reminds us that her own private agony is more important to her than the rest of the world's business. Thus Miss Havisham asserts her formidable personal power when she stretches out her hand to Pip as he begins the second phase of his great expectations.

Herbert Pocket unknowingly hits on exactly the right name for Pip when Pocket elects to call him "Handel." Pip has been "handled" by Miss Havisham, Magwitch, Mrs. Joe, Pumblechook, and even Joe. Pip has only just encountered Jaggers, whose manipulative ability matches Miss Havisham's. As Herbert intends, the nickname accounts as well for Pip's anomalous position as both a former blacksmith and a newly made member of the upper class. In his innocence, Pip risks being roughly handled by the shadier members of his new class, but in fact his circle of acquaintances includes only a few villainous sorts. Most of Pip's misfortunes have their origins in his youth. The change of scene to London does not introduce many new characters to Pip's psychic play. Drummle seems like an upper-class version of Orlick, and a less interesting one, except in one respect. The one exception is Drummle's marriage to Estella, so painful to Pip that he remains relatively reticent about it in his narrative, considering its importance both to Pip and to his readers. He cannot bear to dwell on it. Drummle becomes Pip's (successful) sexual rival, and Pip cannot easily admit to himself, let alone his readers, that he has sexual feelings for Estella.

London does not match the marsh country in its demons and witches of the first water. Orlick, Miss Havisham, Pumblechook, Mrs. Joe—these are the potent figures in Pip's life, and they all hail from his childhood. In fact, Pip was a child when he began his relationship with Jaggers as well. They all seem to partake of the peculiar potency of Pip's childhood fancies; when Pip matures and goes to cosmopolitan London, he finds fewer monsters and more men. The highly dramatic scenes in the latter two-thirds of the book occur during Pip's frequent visits to the marsh country. Only the reunion with Magwitch and his death occur in London, events in any case inextricably linked with Pip's childhood.

One exception is Jaggers' formidable housekeeper, Molly. Jaggers calls

Pip's attention to her wrists, to the power palpable in her scarred forearms. As Pip learns from Wemmick later, Jaggers' gesture of dominance over the woman, meant to enhance his own power in the eyes of his guests, involves an indirect boast. Molly's case was Jaggers' first great success as a lawyer, and he won his victory by underplaying the strength of her hands. Thus begins Pip's unconscious search for the connection he feels but cannot articulate between Molly's hand gesture and someone else's. In the end, of course, Pip realizes that Molly and Estella have a similar way of moving their hands and deduces from his observation that Molly must be Estella's mother.

Unlike Molly, Wemmick has no hands. Both Jaggers and Wemmick carefully maintain the latter's subservient role and their reserved, professional relationships, despite Wemmick's abilities and seniority in the firm. Wemmick refuses to take responsibility for or control of others' actions, and his hands are not mentioned. He simply advises Pip to take hold of all "portable property," and his hands remain up his sleeves.

Only during two episodes do Wemmick's hands come out of his sleeves. The first concerns his courtship and marriage to Miss Skiffins. The sly journey of Wemmick's hands around the waist of the prim lady and her repulsion of his advances tell the tale of the eventually successful and always proper wooing. The other occasion comes when Wemmick asserts himself in the effort to spirit Magwitch out of the country before the creatures of justice catch him. Wemmick provides much practical help and useful advice to the principals during their adventures. The emergence of Wemmick's hands from the impersonal safety of his sleeves thus reliably signals self-assertion or aggressive activity on his part.

Both Miss Havisham's and Estella's hands prove equally revealing as Pip begins to disclose the two women's secrets. Pip knows that knowledge in his world translates into power; thus we may understand the motivation that drives him to uncover Estella's sordid past. Unable to win from her even the equivocal control that returned affection bestows, Pip resorts to detective work as a substitute. If he cannot have Estella, in short, at least he may discover all that he can about her. In chapter 44, then, after he has learned the discouraging secret of the source of his wealth, Pip returns to Satis House to confront its two inhabitants and try to wring a confession of love from either of them. He fails with both women, at least at the time. Estella's hands work busily and complacently throughout Pip's impassioned speech, the provoking calmness of her hands seeming to mock the sincerity of Pip's outburst. Unmoved by his passion, Estella deliberately and cruelly informs him that she will soon marry Drummle, the worst possible choice Pip could imagine. Her hands stop knitting only once during the entire scene:

> "You cannot love him, Estella?"
> Her fingers stopped for the first time, as she retorted rather angrily, "What

have I told you? Do you think, in spite of it, that I do not mean what I say?"

"You would never marry him, Estella?"

She looked toward Miss Havisham, and considered for a moment with her work in her hands. Then she said, "Why not tell you the truth? I am going to be married to him." (P. 344)

The only emotion that she finally reveals is irritation at having to explain herself and at Pip's obstinacy in refusing to stop loving her. Far from being flattered, Estella merely wishes in a cold way that Pip would not damage himself by constantly wrecking his love on the obdurate rocks of her indifference. In the context, then, Estella's considering "for a moment with her work in her hands" takes on more meanings than just the immediate one. She looks to Miss Havisham but initiates the revelation about her marriage on her own. In marrying, Estella takes her life into her own hands, leaving the tutelage of Miss Havisham in the past. One guesses from Miss Havisham's reaction that marriage to Drummle is not her idea. The culmination of her plans would involve crushing some successful man's heart just as her own has been crushed, and both we and she suspect that Drummle has little heart to crush. Estella has defied Miss Havisham by deliberately throwing herself away on a brute to show her contempt for all that Miss Havisham has done for her and further to show her contempt for herself. Such self-hatred strikes the reader ultimately as a form of suicide.

Miss Havisham reveals her own attitude toward what she has done in her last scene with Pip. She begs forgiveness, and as she does so, her hands once again tell the tale:

> She turned her face to me for the first time since she had averted it, and to my amazement, I may even add to my terror, dropped on her knees at my feet; with her folded hands raised to me in the manner in which, when her poor heart was young and fresh and whole, they must often have been raised to Heaven from her mother's side. . . .
>
> "What have I done! What have I done!" she wrung her hands, and crushed her white hair, and returned to this cry over and over again. "What have I done!" (P. 377)

Finally, their roles are reversed; Pip has become the benefactor and Miss Havisham the supplicant. I think most readers find the scene as startling and dramatic as Pip does. The genius in Miss Havisham's characterization shows most clearly here, when she acts uncharacteristically. She suddenly becomes human where she had seemed witchlike, in the process of disclosing the secret of her adult life. While stealing Estella's heart away and putting ice in its place, the old woman herself has fallen in love with Estella. Miss Havisham is not a mere neurotic shell but a terribly *human* being whose response to her great mistaken love proves to be loving again.

Her revelation of remorse marks the shift in power between Pip and Miss Havisham. By acknowledging regret, Miss Havisham reveals herself to be a participant in the moral order of *Great Expectations*, in which guilt for mistaken love must be expiated.

The sudden conflagration that threatens to consume Miss Havisham provides the vengeance that the moral order of the novel must exact, and the penance that Miss Havisham has newly expressed the need to pay.[6] But Pip demonstrates to the reader that his recently won power over Miss Havisham has not come without cost. He plunges into the flames, ostensibly to save Miss Havisham, acquiring severe burns on his hands. The language of hands unmistakably signals to us that Pip punishes himself for taking control in the relationship with Miss Havisham. He subconsciously attempts to destroy the hands that, in the symbolic language of the novel, are his instruments of power.

One might think that one such ritual gesture of self-effacement and expiation of guilt would suffice. The gesture is self-emasculatory, because male hands in the novel are in one sense extensions of phallic power. Pip's guilt centers on his sexual feelings for Estella, of which Pip is afraid Miss Havisham will disapprove; in this context we may consider the sudden appearance of Orlick at Satis House. Pip's indignation at Orlick's position comes largely, I think, from his fear that Estella will be degraded by Orlick's presence. Pip expresses, however, only the more easily voiced objection about Orlick's general unsuitability. But Orlick (like Uriah in *David Copperfield*) has dogged the hero's tracks throughout his sexual career.[7] Orlick voices his lust for Biddy when Pip first becomes aware of her as a friend. Orlick appears again at Satis House when Pip woos Estella as a young man; again, the villain expresses unacceptable thoughts about his prospects in life. As he says, "Ah, young master, there's more changes than yours" (P. 220). The narrator shifts his own sexual longings onto his *doppelgänger,* Orlick. The device makes the journeyman at once an object of sexual jealousy and an easy target. Orlick has access to Biddy and Estella, but both women would find him repulsive as a sexual partner. Thus Pip deflects some of his own energies, making his now sanitized, romantic sentiments acceptable to a (by our standards) sexually reticent Victorian audience.[8]

So strongly do Pip's emotions seize him, however, that even the combined penance of self-immolation and identification with Orlick does not suffice. One more spectacular punishment remains, in which Orlick again figures prominently. Again, too, the language of hands in the scene guides us through the emotional maze in which Pip at once conceals and reveals his self-doubts. Pip receives a suspicious note and, despite his burned condition and the suspect nature of the note, decides to investigate. His credulity indicates his predisposition toward further self-punishment. Once in the limekiln, Pip runs afoul of Orlick, who causes the hero "exquisite pain" by pinning his arms to his sides, rendering him helpless (P. 401). Throughout the scene, Orlick's hands receive prominent mention, as he tortures the narrator. Pip's own hands cause him great agony because of their burnt condition. The narrator dwells on Pip's terrible state with such relish that the self-punishing aspect of the scene cannot escape the reader.

> Faint and sick with the pain of my injured arm, bewildered by the surprise, and yet conscious how easily this threat [of murder] could be put in execution, I desisted, and tried to ease my arm were it ever so little. But it was bound too tight for that. I felt as if, having been burnt before, it were now being boiled. (P. 401)

The distinction between "burnt" and "boiled" gives the prose an almost precious quality. The narrator has become a connoisseur of pain. Orlick's hands and Pip's hands together become instruments for Pip's punishment. Orlick rages about their rivalry, Pip's supposed interference in his life, and the attempted murder of Mrs. Joe. Orlick tries to blame Pip for the last, claiming that Pip set Mrs. Joe on him constantly. The reader receives Orlick's accusations skeptically. The murder weapon provides, however, at once a tangible and symbolic link between the two former apprentices, because Orlick struck Mrs. Joe with Pip's convict's leg iron. A complex chain of guilt thus binds Pip, Magwitch, and Orlick together. Pip derives his guilty identity in part from the convict and uses Orlick as a convenient bogeyman on which to unload his own unacceptable, aggressive emotions. Their childhood relationship as fellow workers at the forge provides the necessary tangible link for Pip to make the psychic, symbolic connection. He uses Orlick to punish characters he believes need punishment, including himself.

Pip emerges from his orgy of self-punishment apparently cleansed and certainly exhausted. His sickness confines him to bed for weeks, and his eventual recovery seems like a rebirth. But to what sort of life will he return? The dozen years or so in business he dismisses in several sentences—Pip's professional life does not hold him (or us) for long. The second ending of the novel comes like a coda to a mournful symphony. One wonders what material the composer will employ from his emotional remnants to shape a final order. Once again, the imagery of hands shows us what possibility for a final reconciliation there may yet be for Pip:

> "We are friends," said I, rising and bending over her, as she rose from the bench.
> "And will continue friends apart," said Estella.
> I took her hand in mine, and we went out of the ruined place; and as the morning mists had risen long ago when I first left the forge, so, the evening mists were rising now, and in all the broad expanse of tranquil light they showed to me, I saw no shadow of another parting from her. (P. 460)

The mists rise in *Great Expectations*, as the narrator hints, whenever the hero begins a new chapter of his life. Despite the ambiguity of the phrasing, then, we have every reason to believe that Estella and Pip will have some sort of life together. But the language of the hands tells us something more definite. When we consider the enormous emotional energy that Pip has devoted throughout the novel to his hands and to the hands of others, the apparently simple phrase, "I took her hand in mine," takes on broad significance. The same hands that join unobtrusively together at the end of the novel began Pip's and Estella's tortured relationship many years before. Pip's "coarse hands" seemed ludicrously common to Estella then. Her hands, of course, were fine and white, a lady's. The comparison caused the sensitive lad much agony. The comparison further delineated the boundaries of their relationship, suggesting limits that the would-be lover found oppressive but that merely amused Estella. Behind the two children the spectral figure of Miss Havisham loomed, working her own hands, manipulating, seeking revenge.

Pip finds himself manipulated by other hands than hers during the course of his life. Jaggers, Mrs. Joe, Pip's trio of benefactors, Joe, Magwitch, and Pumblechook—all these have a hand in Pip's upbringing. Now Pip wants his readers to believe that he has healed himself, that he has learned to manipulate others as he has been manipulated. Standing over Estella, he takes her hand and she does not protest. The tranquility of the surrounding scene attests to the internal peace Pip wants us to believe he has won. He does not take Estella's hand in a frenzy of romantic passion. The quiet mood of the garden suggests an altered relationship. Pip takes Estella's hand aware of the crippled soul with which he links himself. She may have learned from the harrowing experiences of her marriage; more likely, she remains frozen in the bizarre childhood Miss Havisham gave her.

If the last moments of the novel fail to convince readers, leaving them with a nagging sense that the initial, bleaker ending to the novel remains the more appropriate one, that belief may be strengthened by the language of hands in the last scene.[9] By making one aware of the psychic growth that Pip claims to have accomplished as he authoritatively grasps Estella's hand in the ruined garden, the imagery of hands may encourage incredulity in the skeptical reader. Further, one's recent memory of the guilt-ridden scenes in the limekiln and at Satis House may compound one's feeling that Pip's claim of psychic health rests on uncertain ground. Has Pip in fact liberated himself from the past, or has he only placated for the moment those ever-present demons of guilt and memory? I think the nagging doubt cannot be explained away; the mere presence of the two endings themselves gives rise to uncertainty. The canceled ending describes a parting and a final misunderstanding about the child Pip has in tow. In this version, then, the novel ends with confusion, and the uncertainty is reflected in the handshake the two exchange. Pip finds Estella's "touch" reassuring, but mutual understanding comes too late: "suffering . . . had given her a heart to understand what my heart used to be." No matter how ringing the second conclusion, then, the very existence of the first robs the former of its authority. The issue will remain forever moot. But Pip's hands tell us that *he* fully believes in his authority over Estella and in the muted affirmation of the second conclusion. If we choose to remain skeptical, we must be aware that we do so because of our own reluctance to credit Pip's self-proclaimed psychic achievements. The language of the hands informs us that narrator and hero are one at the end of the novel. Pip believes in himself. He has declared a truce with himself by which he will live henceforth.

iii

As we have seen, *Great Expectations* concerns itself above all with the exercise of power in personal relationships. Pip as narrator wants to retain his hold on our affections; he keeps his own desires for power decidedly muted and is quick to show himself as a victim. From Pip's Pumblechooked youth, through his misguided young adulthood, to the maturity of the narrator, the novel investigates the cost in personal agony that manipulation and insensitivity such as Pip experiences incur. But the novel finally pits Jaggers' sophisticated, amoral London against Joe's simple, Christian forge. It is the traditional split between the wicked city and the well-behaved country, but with a difference. *Great Expectations* only glorifies the quaint in a superficial way. Jaggers' London emerges as the stronger force in the novel; the only memory that Joe's forge produces is the song, "Old Clem," which Pip transplants to Satis House. So absence swallows up that bit of Pip's memory of Joe as well, and Jaggers' power endures.

Leaving Joe behind on the road to London, Pip condemns himself to play the appealing victim during the greater part of the novel. He is, in fact, too inexperienced to control his own life. At first, indeed, his role of manufactured gentleman parallels disturbingly the Frankenstein story—the ultimate victim. Magwitch explicitly sounds the theme on his return to London, when he exults in the creation of a gentleman all his own. But Pip demonstrates the danger of such a creation—its tendency to turn on its maker—when he creates a junior Monster of his own, the Avenger. The Avenger makes Pip's life miserable. Like Pip, the Avenger serves no useful purpose, and the master struggles desperately to find things for the boy to do, a comic example of purposeless power. In a more serious vein, Miss Havisham has created another Monster in Estella, seeking to control where she has been controlled. The whole novel in this sense turns on Miss Havisham's eerie phrase, "I stole her heart away and put ice in its place" (P. 378). The two Monsters, Estella and Pip, perfectly suit one another. Thus we have another reason for the inevitability of their union.

What makes Pip a latter-day Monster, we should not forget, is his great expectations—his bid for power and prestige. In this respect too Pip has several imitators, all of whom comment ironically on Pip's performance. When Orlick moves to Satis House, he claims a similarity to Pip, saying, "There's more changes than yours" (P. 220). Mrs. Pocket makes her own life and the life of her family miserable with her version of great expectations. She never lets anyone forget that she should have married better than she did. Mr. Wopsle endures ridicule and poverty in his vain pursuit of thespian great expectations. Finally, Bently Drummle, Pip's Mr. Hyde along with Orlick, is introduced to us as the "next heir but one to a baronetcy" (P. 181). Each of these characters demonstrates the dangers inherent in deciding that life owes one a living. Each fulfills Pip's own fears about what he himself might have become.

One of Magwitch's utterances during his last moments with Pip on the river contradicts Pip's claims for muted happiness with Estella at the end of *Great Expectations*. What Magwitch says is in fact dangerous for Pip to hear, because it argues for an antibourgeois way of life to which Pip might possibly have sunk in his worst moments (by his middle-class lights), utterly overthrowing his great expectations. Magwitch muses:

> "We'd be puzzled to be more quiet and easy-going than we are at present. But—it's a flowing so soft and pleasant through the water, P'rhaps, as makes me think it—I was a thinking through my smoke just then, that we can no more see to the bottom of the next few hours, than we can see to the bottom of this river what I catches hold of. Nor yet we can't no more hold their tide than I can hold this. And it's run through my fingers and gone, you see!" holding up his dripping hand. (P. 415)

Magwitch's rudimentary thinking suggest a *carpe diem* philosophy that Pip in his garden of long-delayed and uncertain happiness would have difficulty adopting, though Magwitch's implicit resignation might (dangerously) appeal to him. But Pip never forgets, and does not let the reader forget, that Magwitch remains a sinner of a high order. A hardened convict, a returned transport, and a would-be murderer, Magwitch in Pip's eyes *does* need the forgiveness Pip bestows on him during his last illness in the prison hospital.[10] If Pip's words over Magwitch's body ("O Lord, be merciful to him a sinner!") (P. 436) seem self-righteous considering Pip's role in the convict's escape, we must remember the social gulf that exists between the two men, which Pip needs desperately to maintain. Magwitch's escape is one more crime in a long succession. Magwitch has much to pray for in

Pip's eyes. The *carpe diem* philosophy that the convict espouses both grows out of and helps perpetuate the very life for which Magwitch must beg forgiveness according to the moral and social order of *Great Expectations*.

At their last interview before Pip leaves the country, Pip and Estella exchange heated words over her impending marriage to the "stupid brute" Drummle (P. 345). Estella responds: "'Don't be afraid of my being a blessing to him,'... 'I shall not be that. Come! Here is my hand. Do we part on this, you visionary boy—or man?'" (P. 345) Offering her hand in a gesture of equality, she modifies her description of Pip as a visionary boy, calling him instead a man. Pip confesses his love during the scene, and Estella acknowledges with these words that his childhood infatuation has grown into something more serious. But she acknowledges more than this at the same time.

Pip, to Estella, must indeed have seemed a strange and "visionary" boy. To an egotist like her, the insecure, lower-class boy who nonetheless possesses a rich inner life must be incomprehensible. Pip's visions are, of course, an important sign for him of the validity of his claims for a higher social status, and Estella's hand in marriage. By "visionary," too, Estella simply means given to seeing visions of love where none exists. Cold as she is, Estella has found and continues to find Pip's talk of love mere moonbeams. But her comment more accurately characterizes Pip's inner life than she realizes.

From his earliest remembered moments, Pip is a teller of tales. He makes stories up about the gravestones of his mother and father, he finds tales in the mists and dykes of the marshes, and he responds with prodigious lies when pushed on the subject of the mysterious Miss Havisham by Mrs. Joe and Uncle Pumblechook. Walking among the dilapidated buildings and ruined gardens of Satis House, Pip has a vision of the death of Miss Havisham, a vision repeated compulsively when he walks in the garden again after his last visit with her.

One of the simplest ways to create a story is by repetition of characters, scenes, or gestures. By repetition, we make sense of the world and remember the stories we hear about it. *Great Expectations* proceeds by repetition; the novel helps the reader follow its episodic plot by repeating characters, scenes, and gestures. The villain of Pip's childhood, Orlick, reappears in the hero's maturity. Characters such as the Avenger, Drummle, Mrs. Pocket, Orlick, and Estella mimic Pip with their great expectations, or in their roles as created Monsters. The authority figures of Pip's youth either reappear later in his life or are mirrored by the authority figures who control Pip as a young man. Pip's awkward behavior on arriving in London is echoed by Joe's equally inept behavior when he visits Pip. Both are disasters at the dinner table. The convict eats like a wolf in front of young Pip, and again when Pip has become a snob in London. Pip attends performances by the great Wopsle twice, helps an escaped convict twice, assists Herbert in business by advancing capital twice, and makes two visits to Walworth that he recounts in detail. Finally, the obsessive repetition of hand gestures lies at the imaginative center of Pip's telling of his *Great Expectations*. He repeats because he must to tell us his tale. The autobiographical format necessarily involves repetition, because the narrator must live his life before he may tell it. The very narrative becomes the first repetition.

The teller of tales finally remains inaccessible to us, at least in part. He cannot disclose all his secrets. Further, his soul is Protean. A teller of tales lives more than one life at the same time. Pip plays the role of a black-smith's apprentice, an idle gentleman, and a businessman. Simultaneous-ly, Pip has recorded all that he has seen, a detached observer of his own experiences. Pip's attempts to settle on a name at the beginning of the novel, and the several nicknames that other characters adopt for him as he grows older—Pumblechook's "Squeaker," Herbert's "Handel," even Joe's "Sir"— indicate, I think, something of that Protean nature. Pip succumbs to an indeterminacy of character that leaves him open to the idea that he may be the hero of his own novel in the first place, that he may record and retell his life as he lives it. The visionary boy who engages his readers at the opening of *Great Expectations* undergoes many transformations dur-ing the long course of his self-revelations.

At the same time, however, some part of him does not change. The same obsession that drives Pip to tell us about the characters he sees on his par-ents' gravestones remains with him at the end, at his inevitable return to the ruined garden in the last chapter. The visionary boy recounts his visions still, telling us that he sees "no shadow of another parting" from Estella. From that part of himself that induces him to narrate his curious tale there can be no parting either.

As readers of *Great Expectations*, finally, we find ourselves caught in the repetitive act of reading; we bring Pip to life and make him tell us his story yet again. We are in Pip's hands and at the same time we have made his tale a part of us. To forget Pip and *Great Expectations* is to forget that place within ourselves where memory abides and where the demons of childhood lurk, forever potent, awaiting our return.

6

Conclusion

> "Stranger,
> you must come from the other end of nowhere,
> else you are a great booby, having to ask
> what place this is. It is no nameless country.
> Why, everyone has heard of it, the nations
> over on the dawn side, toward the sun,
> and westerners in cloudy lands of evening.
> No one would use this ground for training horses,
> it is too broken, has no breadth of meadow;
> but there is nothing meager about the soil,
> the yield of grain is wondrous, and wine too,
> with drenching rains and dewfall.
> There's good pasture
> for oxen and for goats, all kinds of timber,
> and water all year long in the cattle ponds.
> For these blessings, friend, the name of Ithaka
> has made its way even as far as Troy—
> and they say Troy lies far beyond Akhaia."
>
> Homer, *Odyssey* 13.234–49

The methodology I established in my opening chapter sacrifices the reductive coherence of many Dickensian studies for the chance to approximate an individual experience of reading Dickens more closely than before. Such an enterprise must make suspect a final chapter entitled, "Conclusion," because, logically speaking, the work itself essentially constitutes its conclusion. Nonetheless the form of literary criticism demands some sort of closure, however, else readers will echo Mr. Weller, Sr., wondering "vether it's worth while goin' through so much, to learn so little, as the charity-boy said ven he got to the end of the alphabet. . . . *I* rayther think it isn't."[1] The need for a conclusion at the end of a critical work seems to resemble the need even sophisticated readers have for some sort of conclusion at the end

Charles Dickens
ca. 1860

of a Victorian novel. Readers like to know where they have been and how far they have come. My attention to the relationship between narrator and reader in the experience of reading Dickens permits me, moreover, to suggest something of the development of that relationship over the span of Dickens's literary career. If one cannot unlock any secret doors or reveal any sacred mysteries at the center of the Dickens world after a study such as this one, one can delineate large patterns of change in the temporary unions of writer and reader that give life to literary artifacts.

In *The Old Curiosity Shop*, the narrator offers a secondary dialectic that counters the primary moral struggle between Little Nell and Daniel Quilp, between purity and corruption. In opposition to the strong wish to die that both Quilp and Nell finally evince, the narrator offers nascent communities in the shape of pairs of characters who form lasting bonds of mutual dependence. The narrator seems to reassure the reader that, despite the destruction of the main characters, creation still has a place. The fancy that produces so much creation and so much destruction celebrates its power in the relationship between narrator and reader by, in effect, taking the novelistic world apart and putting it back together again. The reader witnesses a wild glee in Quilp's most entertainingly destructive moments that we might almost confuse with creativity, so ingenious is it.

But sharp limits exist in this dialogue of creative and destructive power. The narrator draws clear moral lines between the sinful Quilp who dies a miserable, nihilistic death, and the pure Little Nell, who dies amidst mourners on earth to regret her going and Angels in the air to point the way to heaven. The extreme distinctions that the narrator makes suggest that he is much concerned with firmly rejecting the imp of evil lest Quilp seduce even him. The dwarf's potency and manic energy threaten to become dangerously appealing. *The Old Curiosity Shop* reveals to the reader a narrator uncertain of the moral cost of creative output yet determined within certain bounds to explore the seamier sides of creativity. We sense as readers that such a narrator may never understand the deepest levels of criminal motivation because of his unwillingness to set aside his moral blinders to see more fully. The narrator's prodigious creative powers do allow him, however, to examine the criminal mind with powerful, if narrow, precision.

In *David Copperfield*, an uneasy balance has been struck between the evil forces in the novel such as Uriah Heep and the forces of good, embodied in Agnes. Darker shadows exist at the edges of that cheerful, well-lit hearth over which Agnes presides; only the narrator's insistence banishes Uriah from that charmed circle. One senses that if the narrator let his guard down even for a moment, Uriah would appear at the doorstep of the Copperfield cottage, in disguise, selling fraudulent landshares or the like.

But the moral issues, though still central to the novel, have given way to an unexpected development in the narrator's art. Agnes's role in the novel is to provide David with the discipline he needs to put his fancy to commercial use in novel writing. The dialectical struggle here between discipline and fancy shifts the moral emphasis in *The Old Curiosity Shop* from the fate of good and evil in the world of Victorian England to the battle in one man's soul to triumph over his more ignoble tendencies. Further, an interesting shift in the moral valences of the dialectical equation has occurred. If Nell has grown up a little to become Agnes, then the former's purity has become the self-discipline that Agnes possesses from the start and that David must find. Moreover, though Quilp has been sacrificed on some sexual altar for the sake of repression, his evil creativity has become the fancy by which David must live. Thus it seems to me that the narrator indicates a surprisingly ambivalent attitude toward the very creativity that makes him who he is. Moreover, the narrator's ambivalence reveals a genuine internal contradiction in *David Copperfield*. The text wants both ends of the polarity it has established: the passion of creativity and the productivity of self-discipline. David remains incomplete as a character until his union with Agnes. His fancy requires her discipline; alone, David drifts aimlessly, succumbing to mild self-indulgences such as drink and theater-going. Thus comparing the change in the narrator's attitudes toward his central characters between the two novels reveals an uneasy moral identification of the darker side of the creative urge with self-indulgence, excess, and ultimately evil itself.

The narrator's moral evaluation of his art has become less severe at the writing of *Little Dorrit*. The apparently sharp lines drawn between the authorities in the novel that imprison its characters and the fancy that keeps them alive put the sympathy clearly on the side of the victims. Our close examination of the dialectic in *Little Dorrit* shows, however, that once again a final balance in the novel is not so easily found. The fancy that keeps Clennam alive as a child under the harsh domination of his mother threatens to bring him ultimately to suicide as a man. The authority that many of the characters find so irksome, so restrictive in their daily lives, creates the grounds on which fancy may play most vigorously. The most energetic satire in *Little Dorrit* comes at the expense of the most restrictive authorities: the Circumlocution Office, Mrs. Merdle's Society, Casby's Patriarchal Benevolence.

Fancy in *Little Dorrit* further may tend to perpetuate the very role of victim, by making it bearable for one like Clennam.[2] In other words, Clennam's fancy enables him to continue in the passive life he leads as a child under his mother's rule. His fancy further tends to ensure that Clennam will repeat the performance as a man. The narrator shows at once a greater sympathy for and a deeper understanding of the ambiguous position fancy holds in the Dickensian universe. The narrator's vision has turned outward toward his entire society, but in the process, he has deepened his insight into the individual workings of a mind like Arthur Clennam's or Little Dorrit's.

The demons of childhood lurk at the center of the obsessive mysteries that the narrator of *Great Expectations* alternately conceals from and reveals to the readers. Pip, the "visionary boy" of the marshes, lives stubbornly within a self-created realm of fancy that protects him from the disappointments of reality outside. The tale of his great expectations is the tale of many seductive confirmations of his visions. His secretive nature, given to obsessive repetitions of his concerns, nonetheless inadvertently reveals some of its deepest secrets in the language of hands in the novel. Fancy has almost completely triumphed over any external authority in *Great Expectations*. Only a central weakness ultimately gives the game away: Pip's guilty connection to the convict proves to be his downfall, as far as his self-contained world of fancy is concerned. In the last scene of the novel, however, fancy demonstrates its durability, and its stubbornness, in holding on to what remains of the childish, romantic dream of love with Estella. The apparent serenity of *Great Expectations* masks, then, a desperate struggle at a deep level of the soul between the authority of reality and a fancy that largely refuses to compromise.

Tracing patterns of development in a pluralistic universe runs the risk of imposing an attractive order on an unwieldy chaos. Yet I believe that the dialectical arguments put forth here recreate in a dynamic way the (limiting) experience of a particular reading of the Dickensian novel. We do not make the mistake of generalizing the study of the interchange between narrator and reader to include some historical reconstruction of Dickens's psyche, or his own emotional development, or the like. Studying the experience of reading Dickens's novels does not permit us to perform such leaps of faith. Nor do we need to; I think the aims of criticism have been served if one has learned something more about what it means to sit down with a book like *The Old Curiosity Shop* or *Great Expectations*.[3]

Finally, as twentieth-century readers of nineteenth-century novels, we can see from the foregoing discussion that reading the fiction of the past does not consist of the "free play" that critics often assert it does.[4] These novels guide us into making moral decisions about characters, situations, and events that have largely predetermined outcomes. The Dickensian universe is one in which moral evaluations constantly are made, indeed constantly must be made in order fully to participate in the reading of the fiction. The four novels we have studied dictate to us the terms of victory and surrender in the moral battles that rage between their covers. Nowhere can fancy play without restriction; it draws its very life, indeed, from the struggle to maintain its integrity within imposed boundaries. Reading these books, we undertake a journey with clear moral signposts to point the way. In the Dickensian novel, even one's dreams must submit to the moral scrutiny that begins so much of the action and so much of the agony that fills these inexhaustible fictions.

Notes

Chapter 1. Critical Issues

1. I am drawing here on Wolfgang Iser, *The Act of Reading: A Theory of Aesthetic Response* (Baltimore: Johns Hopkins University Press, 1979) and Martin Heidegger, *Being and Time* (New York: Harper and Row, 1962) for these arguments.
2. Paul B. Armstrong, *The Challenge of Bewilderment: Understanding and Representation in James, Conrad, and Ford* (Ithaca: Cornell University Press, 1987), P. 18.
3. For the view that champions criticism and the critic over the work of art, see Harold Bloom, *The Anxiety of Influence: A Theory of Poetry* (London: Oxford University Press, 1975); *A Map of Misreading* (New York: Oxford University Press, 1975); *The Breaking of the Vessels* (Chicago: University of Chicago Press, 1982); and Moynihan, Robert, ed., *A Recent Imagining: Interviews with Harold Bloom, Geoffrey Hartman, J. Hillis Miller, Paul De Man* (Hamden, CT: Archer Books, 1986).
4. From James's review of *Our Mutual Friend*, quoted in Philip Collins, ed., *Dickens: The Critical Heritage* (London: Routledge and Kegan Paul, 1971).
5. *Edmund Dulac's Fairy-Book: Fairy Tales of the Allied Nations* (1915; reprint, New York: Portland House, 1988). For an account of the origin of *Pickwick Papers*, see Fred Kaplan, *Dickens: A Biography* (New York: William Morrow, 1988), Pp. 76–84.
6. Many sources might be cited here. For example, Walter Houghton, *The Victorian Frame of Mind* (New Haven: Yale University Press, 1957).
7. Cf. Paul Fussell, *The Great War and Modern Memory* (London: Oxford University Press, 1975), and Fussell, *Thank God for the Atom Bomb and Other Essays* (New York: Summit Books, 1988).
8. Cf. Bruno Bettlheim, *The Uses of Enchantment: The Meaning and Importance of Fairy Tales* (New York: Knopf, 1976).
9. For example, see Jacques Derrida, *L'ecriture et la difference* (1967; reprint, Paris: Editions du Seuil, 1979) or *Glas*, trans. John P. Leavey, Jr., and Richard Rand (Lincoln: University of Nebraska Press, 1986).
10. I am judging roughly by the decrease in "deconstructive" papers in mainline journals like *PMLA*, and by the increase in arguments to the contrary in many critical books and reviews. Cf. n. 12.
11. For example, see Barbara Herrnstein Smith, *Contingencies of Value: Alternative Perspectives for Critical Theory* (Cambridge: Harvard University Press, 1989).
12. John M. Ellis, *Against Deconstruction* (Princeton: Princeton University Press, 1989), P. 118.
13. Ludwig Wittgenstein, *On Certainty,* ed. G. E. M. Anscombe and G. H. von Wright (1969; reprint, New York: Harper and Row, 1972), P. 2e.

14. Wittgenstein, *On Certainty*, Pp. 10e, 24e, 67e.
15. Cf. John Kucich, "Narrative Theory as History: A Review of Problems in Victorian Fiction Studies," *Victorian Studies* 28, no. 4 (Summer 1985): 657–675, and Linda Alcoff, "Cultural Feminism versus postStructuralism: The Identity Crisis in Feminist Theory," *Signs* 13, no. 3 (Spring 1988): 405–437, both of whom call attention to the ongoing philosophical debate over scepticism in their respective camps.
16. For example, see Karen Offen, "Defining Feminism: A Comparative Historical Approach," *Signs* 14, no. 1 (Autumn 1988): 119–158, which describes feminism as both political and ideological, and as prowomen but not antimen. See also Alexander Welsh, "The Evidence of Things Not Seen: Justice Stephen and Bishop Butler," *Representations* no. 22 (Spring 1988): 60–89. Welsh brings a host of historical and sociological issues to the literary discussion.
17. Cf. Philip Collins, "Charles Dickens," in *Victorian Fiction: A Second Guide to Research,* ed. George H. Ford (New York: Modern Language Association of America, 1978), Pp. 34–113. Collins also discusses the chaotic state of Dickensian criticism. He makes two specific recommendations from which my argument has benefited. First, he urges future critics to remember that one cannot analyze Dickens's works without understanding the age from which they derive. Second, Collins argues that current criticism too often forgets that Dickens's works cannot be reduced to a single theme; the Dickensian oeuvre remains too multifarious. One might even trace the passion for biographical criticism to Forster, Dickens's first biographer-critic. I start with Chesterton because of the clear influence on him of Dilthey. G. K. Chesterton, *Charles Dickens* (1906; reprint, London: Burns & Oates, 1975).
18. For example, see Edgar Johnson, *Charles Dickens: His Tragedy and Triumph* (New York: Simon and Schuster, 1952).
19. For example, see Barbara Hardy, *The Moral Art of Dickens* (New York: Oxford University Press, 1970). Hardy criticizes Dickens's work for not being as complex, subtle, and indirect as Henry James's. Cf. also John Kucich, "Death Worship Among the Victorians: *The Old Curiosity Shop*," *PMLA* 95, no. 1 (January 1980): 58–73. Kucich tailors Dickens to fit the (then) latest French fashions in philosophy.
20. Humphrey House (London: Oxford University Press, 1950); J. Hillis Miller (Cambridge, MA: Harvard University Press, 1958); Angus Wilson (Hammondsworth, Middlesex, England: Penguin Books, 1972); Andrew Sanders, *Charles Dickens, Resurrectionist* (New York: St. Martins Press, 1982); Taylor Stoehr, *Dickens: The Dreamer's Stance* (Ithaca, NY: Cornell University Press, 1965); Geoffrey Thurley, *The Dickens Myth: Its Genesis and Structure* (London: Routledge and Kegan Paul, 1976); Paul Schlicke, *Dickens and Popular Entertainment* (London: Allen and Unwin, 1985); Robert Garis, *The Dickens Theatre: A Reassessment of the Novels* (London: Oxford University Press, 1965).
21. For example, see James R. Kincaid, *Dickens and the Rhetoric of Laughter* (Oxford: Clarendon Press, 1971). Kincaid, in attempting to correct the view of Dickens as solely a serious social critic, which itself came in reaction to the Pickwickian Dickens, exaggerates once again the humorous aspects of the novels.
22. For example, see Edmund Wilson, "Dickens: The Two Scrooges," in *The Wound and the Bow: Seven Studies in Literature* (New York: Oxford University Press, 1965), Pp. 3, 9–10. Wilson begins the twentieth-century reevaluation of Dickens with this essay, but he himself never gets past his biographical obsession. Like his nineteenth-century predecessors who hunted for the real locales behind the fictive ones in *Pickwick Papers*, Wilson hunts for real people behind the fictional characters. Cf. also Steven Marcus, *Dickens: From Pickwick to Dombey* (New York: Basic Books, 1965). Marcus makes

a poorly resolved Oedipal complex and Dickens's troubles with his father bear the burden of interpretation of the novels from *Pickwick Papers* to *Dombey and Son.*

23. Here I use as a starting point Wolfgang Iser, *The Implied Reader* (Baltimore: Johns Hopkins University Press, 1974), ch. 11, and *The Act of Reading: A Theory of Aesthetic Response* (Baltimore: Johns Hopkins University Press, 1979). We must realize, however, that readers are individuals; there are no ideal readers.

24. Cf. Collins's similar complaint in "Charles Dickens," Pp. 34–113.

25. I am indebted here and in the following paragraphs to the work of Ludwig Wittgenstein. Cf. *Philosophical Investigations,* trans. G. E. M. Anscombe (New York: Macmillan, 1953).

26. Formalist critics and those who make a cult of the critic do exactly this. Cf. n. 3. For Kant, see *Critique of Judgment,* trans. J. H. Bernard (New York: Hafner Press, 1951), bk. 1, Pp. 37–81.

27. Ellis, *The Theory of Literary Criticism: A Logical Analysis* (Berkeley: University of California Press, 1974), P. 44.

28. Cf., for example, Stanley E. Fish, *Self-Consuming Artifacts* (Berkeley: University of California Press, 1972).

29. Cf. Martin Heidegger, *Being and Time,* trans. John Macquarrie and Edward Robinson (New York: Harper and Row, 1962), Pp. 188–195.

30. For the part-whole relationships, see Leo Spitzer, *Linguistics and Literary History* (Princeton: Princeton University Press, 1948), Pp. 1–39. For the hermeneutic circle, Hans Georg Gadamer, *Philosophical Hermeneutics,* trans. David E. Linge (Berkeley: University of California Press, 1976), Pp. 1–104.

31. For example, see E. D. Hirsch, Jr., *Validity in Interpretation* (New Haven: Yale University Press, 1967).

32. The term "fusion" is Gadamer's. Cf. no. 30.

33. *The Interpretation of Dreams,* trans. James Strachey (New York: Basic Books, 1955), was first published in 1899, although Freud had 1900 put on the title page. The gesture neatly captures the sense in which Freud participated in the closing of one era and the opening of another. Cf. also *A General Introduction to Psychoanalysis,* trans. Joan Riviere (New York: Simon and Schuster, 1953).

34. I draw on Paul Ricoeur, *Freud and Philosophy,* trans. Denis Savage (New Haven: Yale University Press, 1970), for the following argument.

35. Here, and in what follows, I employ Ricoeur's terminology of *arche* and *telos.*

36. For example, see Lawrence Jay Dessner, "*Great Expectations:* 'The Ghost of a Man's Own Father,'" *PMLA* 91, no. 3 (May 1976) 436–450.

37. Cf. Soren Kierkegaard, *Fear and Trembling: A Dialectical Lyric,* trans. Walter Lowrie (Princeton: Princeton University Press, 1941).

38. For example, see Fred Kaplan, *Dickens: A Biography* (New York: William Morrow, 1988).

39. Charles Dickens, *The Old Curiosity Shop: The Oxford Illustrated Dickens* (London: Oxford University Press, 1971), P. 13. All subsequent references are to this edition.

40. Charles Dickens, *David Copperfield: The Oxford Illustrated Dickens* (London: Oxford University Press, 1974), P. 697. All subsequent references are to this edition.

Chapter 2. The Angel and the Imp

1. George H. Ford, *Dickens and His Readers* (New York: W. W. Norton, 1965), Pp. 55–71.

2. Hans-Georg Gadamer, *Philosophical Hermeneutics,* trans. David E. Linge (Berkeley: University of California Press, 1976), cf. especially part 1, Pp. 1–4. My analysis of *The Old Curiosity Shop* in terms of merging horizons owes much to Gadamer's work.

3. Cf. Wolfgang Iser, *The Implied Reader* (Baltimore: Johns Hopkins University Press, 1974), Pp. 274–294.

4. Angus Wilson, *The World of Charles Dickens* (Harmondsworth, Middlesex, England: Penguin Books, 1972), P. 138.

5. Dickens, *Old Curiosity Shop,* P. 3.

6. Walter Houghton, *The Victorian Frame of Mind* (New Haven: Yale University Press, 1957), Pp. 341–393.

7. Thomas Carlyle, "Sartor Resartus," *Fraser's Magazine* (London, n. p., 1833–34), bk. 2, chap. 5.

8. Richard D. Altick, *Victorian People and Ideas* (New York: W. W. Norton, 1973), P. 277.

9. Barbara Hardy, *The Moral Art of Dickens* (New York: Oxford University Press, 1970), cf. chap. 1, for example.

10. E. Royston Pike, ed. *Golden Times* (New York: Schocken Books, 1972), Pp. 230–1.

11. Houghton, *Victorian Frame of Mind,* Pp. 341–393.

12. Georges Bataille, *Death and Sensuality* (New York: Walker, 1962), P. 5.

13. Paul Schlicke, *Dickens and Popular Entertainment* (London: Allen and Unwin, 1985), focuses almost exclusively on Punch as Quilp's antecedent and thus misses most of his darker elements.

14. Susan R. Horton, *The Reader in the Dickens World: Style and Response* (London: Macmillan, 1981), argues that the novel pulls the reader away from this central story. I would argue, as must be clear from the foregoing, that Nell and Quilp are precisely the most important and interesting aspects of the novel.

15. Atta Britwum, "Dickens's War against the Militancy of the Oppressed," *Victorian Newsletter* 65 (Spring 1984): 15–19, says, "Dickens is a defender of the bourgeois order" (P. 18). I believe this typical Marxist response is wide of the mark. Dickens's relation to the bourgeois world is far more complex than this.

16. See Jean-Paul Sartre, *Literature and Existentialism,* trans. Bernard Frechtman (Secaucus, NJ: The Citadel Press, 1972), for the idea of reading as a willed, initially free grappling with the demands of a text.

17. See Alexander Welsh, *The City of Dickens* (Oxford: Clarendon Press, 1971), for a discussion of the Victorian city in these terms.

Chapter 3. Doric Dreams

1. Dickens, *David Copperfield,* P. 184.

2. See Geoffrey Thurley, *The Dickens Myth: Its Genesis and Structure* (London: Routledge and Kegan Paul, 1976), Ch. 1, for the idea of identification.

3. Cf. Sigmund Freud, *A General Introduction to Psychoanalysis,* trans. Joan Riviere (New York: Simon and Schuster, 1953), esp. pt. 3, P. 255ff.

4. Philip Collins, in *Dickens: Interviews and Recollections,* 2 vols. (Totowa, NJ: Barnes and Noble, 1981), cites Dickens confessing that he put a good deal of his own childhood in *David Copperfield* (1: 1). Thus, it is perhaps no surprise that it becomes his favorite novel (2: 327, 346). This is well-known; the danger arises when critics try to use the life too literally to force an interpretation of the work.

5. Cf. Ricoeur, *Freud and Philosophy,* Pp. 459–551.

6. Alexander Welsh, *From Copyright to Copperfield: The Identity of Dickens* (Cambridge, MA: Harvard University Press, 1987), pinpoints this disease in Dickens's own life, shifting the emotional "heat" of the novel away from the usual blacking warehouse to a mature Dickens suffering an identity crisis in midlife. Although interesting, this line of reasoning should not keep us from the text itself, lest the argument become a vicious circle of art to life to art and so forth.

7. For example, see Angus Wilson, *The World of Charles Dickens* (Harmondsworth, Middlesex, England: Penguin Books, 1972), Pp. 211–16. U. C. Knoepflmacher, in "The Balancing of Child and Adult: An Approach to Victorian Fantasies for Children," *Nineteenth-Century Fiction* 39, no. 4 (March 1985): 497–530, suggests a more useful dialectic between the special world of the child and the double readership of childhood stories by child and adult. For an overly simplistic, but essentially correct view of Dickens's handling of parents and children, see Arthur A. Adrian, *Dickens and the Parent–Child Relationship* (Athens, OH: Ohio University Press, 1984).

8. Cf. Mark Spilka, *Dickens and Kafka* (Bloomington: Indiana University Press, 1963), the chapter on *David Copperfield*, for discussion of Steerforth's domination of David.

9. See Wolfgang Iser, *The Implied Reader* (Baltimore: Johns Hopkins University Press, 1974), Pp. 274–94, for the idea of gaps.

10. Thurley, ch. 1.

11. Laura Hapke, in "He Stoops to Conquer: Redeeming the Fallen Woman in the Fiction of Dickens, Gaskell and Their Contemporaries," *Victorian Newsletter* 69 (Spring 1986): 16–23, points out that the key to understanding Em'ly's story is acknowledging the importance of the wrath of "respectable women" and the need for a protective male to keep an eye on her as she flees England. It is a valuable account.

12. The dangers of biographical criticism are clear here, for even a cursory familiarity with Dickens's life will reveal as many differences as similarities with the wish fulfillment going on at the end of the novel. Better is Fred Kaplan's discussion, in his excellent *Dickens: A Biography* (New York: William Morrow, 1988), in which he muses on the extent of Dickens's hypochondria as an aspect of his mimetic powers. When writing of David's youth, Dickens again suffered an old pain in his side (Pp. 243–50).

13. See James R. Kincaid, *Dickens and the Rhetoric of Laughter* (Oxford: Clarendon Press, 1971), ch. 7, for the idea of laughter as a means of releasing hostility, fear. The view is ultimately Freudian.

14. John P. McGowan, "David Copperfield: The Trial of Realism," *Nineteenth-Century Fiction* 34, no. 1 (1979): 1–20 argues that *David Copperfield* marks the culmination of the battle between "fancy" and "realism" in Dickens's works. I would respond that Dickens has committed himself to "fancy" (subject to the restraining limits of discipline) long before writing *David Copperfield*. Cf., for example, *The Old Curiosity Shop*.

Chapter 4. In the Prison House of Fancy

1. This view of *Little Dorrit*, which I use as my starting point, was first advanced by J. Hillis Miller in *Charles Dickens: The World of His Novels* (London: Oxford University Press, 1959). It has been more recently argued by Alistair M. Duckworth, "Little Dorrit and the Question of Closure," *Nineteenth-Century Fiction* 33, no. 1, (1978): 110–31. Duckworth's essay ably updates Miller's seminal work.

2. Charles Dickens, *Little Dorrit* (Oxford: Clarendon Press, 1979), P. 741. All subse-

quent references are to this edition.

3. Susan R. Horton, in *The Reader in the Dickens World: Style and Response* (London: Macmillan, 1981), also analyzes the opening, taking Dickens's many metaphors as keys to his interior life. She pushes too hard, I believe, to find biography in the art.

4. Lionel Trilling first made this point in his introduction to the *Oxford Illustrated Dickens* edition of *Little Dorrit* (London: Oxford University Press, 1953).

5. Elaine Showalter, in "Guilt, Authority, and the Shadows of Little Dorrit," *Nineteenth-Century Fiction* 34, no. 1 (1979): 20–40, also notices the contrasts between the initial chapters of books 1 and 2. The larger point, that these contrasts come in a novel of contrasts, that *Little Dorrit* derives its narrative force in large part from the contrasting images that help develop the theme of fancy versus authority in the novel, I have not seen elsewhere.

6. Cf. Altick, *Victorian People and Ideas,* chap. 5.

7. For an excellent discussion of the Victorian city and its satirists' practices, see Alexander Welsh, *The City of Dickens* (Oxford: Clarendon Press, 1971), esp. pt. 1, chap. 1.

8. The notion is common to Freud's thinking on the subject of hysterical diseases and other obsessional behavior; see, for example, *Three Case Histories* (New York: Collier Books, 1963).

9. Guilty of breathtaking historical irrelevancy was Sir James FitzJames Stephens, who attacked the Circumlocution Office and *Little Dorrit* on its publication as follows: "He [Dickens] seems, as a general rule, to get his first notions of an abuse from the discussions which accompany its removal, and begins to open his trenches and mount his batteries as soon as the place to be attacked has surrendered." Quoted in Alan Shelston, ed., *Charles Dickens's Dombey and Son and Little Dorrit: A Casebook* (London: Macmillan, 1985), P. 120. If only governmental red tape had been so permanently cut!

10. John R. Reed, in "A Friend to Mammon: Speculation in Victorian Literature," *Victorian Studies* 27, no. 2 (Winter 1984): 179–203, cites Merdle as the first memorable portrait in Victorian fiction of a speculator.

11. Two contrasting discussions of Little Dorrit's passivity from which this argument has benefited are Alison Booth, "Little Dorrit and Dorothea Brooke: Interpreting the Heroines of History," *Nineteenth-Century Literature* 41, no. 2 (September 1986): 190–216, and Susan K. Gillman and Robert L. Patten, "Dickens:Doubles::Twain: Twins," *Nineteenth-Century Fiction* 39, no. 4 (March 1985): 441–58.

12. I have benefited here from Lynda Zwinger's "The Fear of the Father: Dombey and Daughter," *Nineteenth-Century Fiction* 39, no. 4 (March 1985): 420–41. Her remarks apply well to *Little Dorrit.*

13. Many of Freud's case studies testify to the difficulty he experienced persuading neurotics to relinquish their neuroses. For example, see *Dora: An Analysis of a Case of Hysteria* (New York: Collier Books, 1963).

14. Quoted in Shelston, *Dicken's Dombey and Son,* P. 124.

15. Quoted in Shelston, *Dicken's Dombey and Son,* P. 140.

16. I benefited from Gillman and Patten, "Dickens:Doubles," here. Cf. n. 11.

Chapter 5. A Visionary Boy

1. See Sigmund Freud, *Delusion and Dream and Other Essays*, ed. Philip Reiff (Boston: Beacon Press, 1956), for the idea that we are all artists, fabricators of our own lives.

2. Charles Dickens, *Great Expectations, The Oxford Illustrated Dickens* (London: Oxford

University Press, 1973), P. 1. All subsequent references are to this edition.

3. My argument here parallels that of Charles Forker in "The Language of Hands in *Great Expectations,*" *Texas Studies in Literature and Language* 2, no. 2 (1961): 280–93. I learned of Forker's work only after mine was complete; I did not benefit from his insights in my reading.

4. This reading is in part a corrective to so many critical works that argue that *Great Expectations* is only about money and class. For example, see James M. Brown, *Dickens: Novelist in the Marketplace* (London: Macmillan, 1982).

5. For example, see Wilson, *World of Dickens,* Pp. 268–72.

6. I am indebted to an excellent article by Julian Moynahan, "The Hero's Guilt: The Case of *Great Expectations,*" *Discussions of Charles Dickens,* ed. William Ross Clark (Boston: D. C. Heath and Co., 1961), Pp. 82–93.

7. Once again, I draw on Moynahan, "Hero's Guilt," .

8. The device worked well for both Dickens and his audience, apparently: The novel was both Dickens's favorite after *David Copperfield* and extraordinarily popular with his readers. It sold (in *All the Year Round*) more than 100,000 copies weekly. See Philip Collins, ed., *Dickens: Interviews and Recollections,* 2 vols. (Totawa, NJ: Barnes and Noble, 1981), 1: 163, for the confirmation by Henry Fielding Dickens of Dickens's opinion. See also Robert L. Patten, *Charles Dickens and His Publishers* (Oxford: Clarendon Press, 1978), for the sales figures.

9. One such reader is John Kucich, "Action in the Dickens Ending: *Bleak House* and *Great Expectations,*" *Nineteenth-Century Fiction* 33, no. 1 (1978): 88–110. Kucich argues that Pip in the second ending tries to have his cake and eat it too.

10. Lawrence Jay Dessner, "*Great Expectations*: "'The Ghost of a Man's Own Father,'" *PMLA* 91, no. 3 (1976): 436–50, writes convincingly on Pip's need for Magwitch, though in a heavy-handed, Freudian manner. He misses, oddly enough, the Telemachus connection.

Chapter 6. Conclusion

1. Charles Dickens, *Pickwick Papers, The Oxford Illustrated Dickens* (London: Oxford University Press, 1971), P. 373.

2. Cf. Catherine A. Makinnon, "Feminism, Marxism, Method, and the State: An Agenda for Theory," *Signs* 7 (1982): 515–44. She argues that desire in society is channeled into male potency and female victimization. Here, we can see Dickens slightly expanding those categories.

3. Cf. Michael Slater's otherwise useful work, *Dickens and Women* (Stanford: Stanford University Press, 1983), which breaks new ground analyzing both the women in Dickens's life and in his novels, and only becomes suspect when it forces the connection between the two.

4. Cf. Jacques Derrida, *Glas,* trans. John P. Leavey, Jr., and Richard Rand (Lincoln: University of Nebraska Press, 1986). A more useful attitude is to be found in Mary E. Hawkesworth, "Knowers, Knowing, Known: Feminist Theory and Claims of Truth," *Signs* 14, no. 3 (Spring 1989): 533–58. She argues that, because historical, objective truth is not possible, feminists work toward "situatedness" to explain where they begin, with partial, relative claims on truth. I would only add that this realization should be both freeing and humbling, not a fatal flaw. Indeed, when Derrida strove to undercut the ground of Western philosophy, he purposively tried to leave nowhere to stand. As I have suggested, however, I believe he simply stops at the

wrong point. The question is not where do we stand? Rather, it is how should we act? John Kucick's piece, "Narrative Theory as History: A Review of Problems in Victorian Fiction Studies," *Victorian Studies* 28, no. 4 (Summer 1985): 657–75, has a useful review of the difficulties the so-called new historicism creates when it tries to bring *history* into an argument about the self-referentiality of *texts*. The logical flaw here is indicative of the problem the new historicists have if they simply adopt uncritically certain postmodernist assumptions about language. A good example of someone who falls into this trap is Barbara Herrnstein Smith, *Contingencies of Value: Alternative Perspectives for Critical Theory* (Cambridge, MA: Harvard University Press, 1989), who argues that literary value is radically relative and constantly variable, and thus we should not seek truth but only sociological reportage. The logical jump there indicates the problem: Simply because value is variable, we should not stop doing the best we can to make assessments of value. As I have argued, it is an essential part of our role as critics.

Bibliography

Dickens's Works

Dickens, Charles. *Complete Works* The New Oxford Illustrated Dickens. London: Oxford University Press, 1971.

Collins, Philip, ed. *Charles Dickens: The Public Readings*. Oxford: Clarendon Press, 1975.

Fielding, K. J., ed. *The Speeches of Charles Dickens*. Oxford: Clarendon Press, 1960.

Findlater, Richard, ed. Charles Dickens [ed.] *Memoirs of Joseph Grimaldi*. New York: Stein and Day, 1968 [1838].

House, Madeline, et al., eds. *The Pilgrim Edition of the Letters of Charles Dickens*. Oxford: Clarendon Press, 1965.

Johnson, Edgar, ed. *Letters from Charles Dickens to Angela Burdett-Coutts 1841–1865*. London: Jonathan Cape, 1953.

Stone, Harry, ed. *Charles Dickens' Uncollected Writings from Household Words 1850–1859*. Bloomington: Indiana University Press, 1968.

———. *Dickens' Working Notes for his Novels*. Chicago: University of Chicago Press, 1987.

Tillotson, Kathleen, et al., eds. *Complete Works of Charles Dickens*. Oxford: Clarendon Press, 1979.

Dickensian Criticism

Adrian, Arthur A. *Dickens and the Parent-Child Relationship*. Athens: Ohio University Press, 1984.

Booth, Alison. "Little Dorrit and Dorothea Brooke: Interpreting the Heroines of History" *Nineteenth-Century Literature* 41, no. 2 (September 1986): 190–216.

Britwum, Atta. "Dickens' War Against the Militancy of the Oppressed." *Victorian Newsletter* no. 65 (Spring 1984): 15–19.

Brown, James M. *Dickens: Novelist in the Market-Place*. London: Macmillan, 1982.

Carlisle, Janice. *The Sense of an Audience: Dickens, Thackeray and George Eliot at Mid-Century*. Athens: University of Georgia Press, 1981.

Chancellor, E. Beresford. *Dickens and His Times*. London: Richards, n.d.

Chesterton, G. K. *Charles Dickens*. 1906. Reprint. London: Burns and Oates, 1975.

Clark, Robert. "Riddling the Family Firm: The Sexual Economy in Dombey and Son." *ELH* 51 (1984): 69–84.

Collins, Philip. "Charles Dickens." In *Victorian Fiction: A Second Guide to Research*. Edited by George H. Ford. New York: Modern Language Association of America, 1978, Pp. 34–113.

―――. *Dickens and Crime*. London: Macmillan and Co., 1962.

―――. *Dickens and Education*. London: Macmillan and Co., 1965.

Collins, Philip, ed. *Dickens: The Critical Heritage*. London: , Routledge and Kegan Paul, 1971.

―――. *Dickens: Interviews and Recollections*. 2 vols. Totowa, NJ: Barnes and Noble, 1981.

Daldry, Graham. *Charles Dickens and the Form of the Novel*. London: Croom Helm, 1987.

den Hartog, Dirk. *Dickens and Romantic Psychology*. London: Macmillan, 1987.

Dessner, Lawrence Jay. "*Great Expectations:* 'The Ghost of a Man's Own Father.'" *PMLA* 91, no. 3 (May 1976): 436–50.

Duckworth, Alistair M. "*Little Dorrit* and the Question of Closure." *Nineteenth-Century Fiction* 33, no. 1 (1978): 110–31.

Fido, Martin. *Charles Dickens: An Authentic Account of His Life and Times*. London: Hamlyn, n.d.

Flint, Kate. *Dickens*. Brighton, England: The Harvester Press, 1986.

Ford, George H. *Dickens and His Readers: Aspects of Novel Criticism Since 1836*. New York: W. W. Norton and Co., 1965.

Ford, George H., and Lauriat Lane. *The Dickens Critics*. Westport, CT: Greenwood Press, 1972.

Forker, Charles. "The Language of Hands in *Great Expectations*." *Texas Studies in Literature and Language* 2, no. 2 (Summer 1961).

Forster, John. *The Life of Charles Dickens*. Edited by J. W. T. Ley. London: Cecil Palmer, 1928.

Frank, Lawrence. *Charles Dickens and the Romantic Self*. Lincoln: University of Nebraska Press, 1984.

Garis, Robert. *The Dickens Theatre: A Reassessment of the Novels*. London: Oxford University Press, 1965.

Giddings, Robert, ed. *The Changing World of Charles Dickens*. London: Vision Press, 1983.

Gillman, Susan K. and Robert L. Patten. "Dickens:Doubles::Twain: Twins." *Nineteenth-Century Fiction* 39, no. 4 (March 1985): 441–58.

Goldberg, Michael. *Carlyle and Dickens*. Athens: University of Georgia Press, 1977.

Golding, Robert. *Idiolects in Dickens*. London: Macmillan, 1985.

Grant, Allan. *A Preface to Dickens*. London: Longman, 1984.

Hapke, Laura. "He Stoops to Conquer: Redeeming the Fallen Women in the Fiction of Dickens, Gaskell and Their Contemporaries." *Victorian Newsletter*, no. 69 (Spring 1986): 16–23.

Hardy, Barbara. *Charles Dickens: The Writer and His Work*. Windsor, England: Profile Books, 1983.

―――. *The Moral Art of Dickens*. New York: Oxford University Press, 1970.

Hollington, Michael. *Dickens and the Grotesque*. Totowa, NJ: Barnes and Noble, 1984.

Horton, Susan R. *Interpreting Interpreting: Interpreting Dickens' Dombey*. Baltimore: Johns Hopkins University Press, 1979.

―――. *The Reader in the Dickens World: Style and Response*. London: Macmillan, 1981.

House, Humphrey. *The Dickens World*. 2d ed. London: Oxford University Press, 1970.

Johnson, Edgar. *Charles Dickens: His Tragedy and Triumph*. New York: Simon and Schuster, 1952.

Kaplan, Fred. *Dickens: A Biography*. New York: William Morrow, 1988.

―――. *Dickens and Mesmerism*. Princeton: Princeton University Press, 1975.

Kincaid, James R. *Dickens and the Rhetoric of Laughter*. Oxford: Clarendon Press, 1971.

Kucich, John. "Action in the Dickens Ending: *Bleak House* and *Great Expectations*." *Nineteenth-Century Fiction* 33, no. 1 (1978): 88–110.

―――. "Death Worship among the Victorians: *The Old Curiosity Shop*." *PMLA* 95 no. 1 (January 1980): 58–73.

La Capra, Dominick. "Ideology and Critique in Dickens' *Bleak House*." *Representations* no. 6 (Spring 1984): 116–24.

Lambert, Mark. *Dickens and the Suspended Quotation*. New Haven: Yale University Press, 1981.

Larson, Janet L. *Dickens and the Broken Scripture*. Athens: University of Georgia Press, 1985.

Magnet, Myron. *Dickens and the Social Order*. Philadelphia: University of Pennsylvania Press, 1985.

Marcus, Steven. *Dickens: From Pickwick to Dombey*. New York: Basic Books, 1965.

McGowan, John P. "*David Copperfield:* The Trial of Realism." *Nineteenth-Century Fiction* 34, no. 1 (1979): 1–20.

McMaster, Juliet. *Dickens the Designer*. London: Macmillan, 1987.

Miller, D. A. "Discipline in Different Voices: Bureaucracy, Police, Family, and *Bleak House.*" *Representations* 1, no. 1 (February 1983): 59–91.

Miller, J. Hillis. *Charles Dickens: The World of His Novels*. Cambridge: Harvard University Press, 1958.

Nelson, Harland S. *Charles Dickens*. Boston: Twayne Publishers, 1981.

Newman, S. J. *Dickens at Play*. New York: St. Martin's Press, 1981.

Patten, Robert L. *Charles Dickens and His Publishers*. Oxford: Clarendon Press, 1978.

Perkins, Donald. *Charles Dickens: A New Perspective*. Edinburgh: Floris Books, 1982.

Pickrel, Paul. "*Bleak House:* The Emergence of Theme." *Nineteenth-Century Literature* 42, no. 1 (June 1987): 73–96.

Raina, Badir. *Dickens and the Dialectic of Growth*. Madison: University of Wisconsin Press, 1986.

Romano, John. *Dickens and Reality*. New York: Columbia University Press, 1978.

Rosenberg, Brian. "Physical Opposition in *Barnaby Rudge.*" *Victorian Newsletter* 67 (Spring 1985): 21–23.

Sadoff, Dianne F. *Monsters of Affection: Dickens, Eliot and Bronte on Fatherhood*. Baltimore: Johns Hopkins University Press, 1982.

Sanders, Andrew. *Charles Dickens, Resurrectionist*. New York: St. Martin's Press, 1982.

Sawicki, Joseph. "Oliver (Un)Twisted: Narrative Strategies in *Oliver Twist.*" *Victorian Newsletter* no. 73 (Spring 1988): 23–28.

Schlicke, Paul. *Dickens and Popular Entertainment*. London: Allen and Unwin, 1985.

Senf, Carol A. "*Bleak House:* Dickens, Esther, and the Androgynous Mind." *The Victorian Newsletter* no. 64 (Fall 1983): 21–27.

Shelden, Michael. "Dickens, 'The Chimes,' and the Anti-Corn Law League." *Victorian Studies* 25, no. 3 (Spring 1982): 329–55.

Shelston, Alan, ed. *Charles Dickens' Dombey and Son and Little Dorrit: A Casebook*. London: Macmillan, 1985.

Showalter, Elaine. "Guilt, Authority, and the Shadows of *Little Dorrit.*" *Nineteenth-Century Fiction* 34, no. 1 (1979): 20–40.

Simpson, David. *Fetishism and the Imagination: Dickens, Melville, Conrad*. Baltimore: Johns Hopkins University Press, 1982.

Slater, Michael. *Dickens and Women*. Stanford, CA: Stanford University Press, 1983.

Spilka, Mark. *Dickens and Kafka*. Bloomington: Indiana University Press, 1963.

Steig, Michael. *Dickens and Phiz*. Bloomington: Indiana University Press, 1978.

Stoehr, Taylor. *Dickens: The Dreamer's Stance*. Ithaca, NY: Cornell University Press, 1965.

Stokes, Edward. *Hawthorne's Influence on Dickens and George Eliot*. New York: University of Queensland Press, 1985.

Stone, Harry. *Dickens and the Invisible World: Fairy Tales, Fantasy, and Novel-Making*. London: Macmillan, 1980.

Stone, Marjorie. "Dickens, Bentham, and the Fiction of the Law: A Victorian Controversy and Its Consequences." *Victorian Studies* 29, no. 1 (Autumn 1985): 125–55.

Thomas, Deborah A. *Dickens and the Short Story*. Philadelphia: University of Pennsylvania Press, 1982.

Thurley, Geoffrey. *The Dickens Myth: Its Genesis and Structure*. London: Routledge and Kegan Paul, 1976.

Tsomondo, Thorell. "A Habitable Doll's House: Beginning in *Bleak House*." *The Victorian Newsletter* no. 62 (Fall 1982): 3–7.

Walder, Dennis. *Dickens and Religion*. London: Allen and Unwin, 1981.

Watkins, Gwen. *Dickens in Search of Himself*. London: Macmillan, 1987.

Welsh, Alexander. *From Copyright to Copperfield: The Identity of Dickens*. Cambridge: Harvard University Press, 1987.

———. *The City of Dickens*. Oxford: Clarendon Press, 1971.

Westbury, Barry. *The Confessional Fictions of Charles Dickens*. Dekalb: Northern Illinois University Press, 1977.

Wilson, Angus. *The World of Charles Dickens*. Hammondsworth, England: Penguin Books, 1972.

Wilson, Edmund. "Dickens: The Two Scrooges." *Eight Essays*. New York: Doubleday and Co., 1954.

Wilson, William A. "The Magic Circle of Genius: Dickens' Translations of Shakespearean Drama in *Great Expectations*." *Nineteenth-Century Fiction* 40, no. 2 (September 1985): 154–74.

Zwinger, Lynda. "The Fear of the Father: Dombey and Daughter." *Nineteenth-Century Fiction* 39, no. 4 (March 1985): 420–41.

Other Criticism

Alcoff, Linda. "Cultural Feminism versus Post–Structuralism: The Identity Crisis in Feminist Theory." *Signs* 13, no. 3 (Spring 1988): 405–37.

Armstrong, Nancy. *Desire and Domestic Fiction: A Political History of the Novel*. New York: Oxford University Press, 1987.

Armstrong, Paul B. *The Challenge of Bewilderment: Understanding and Representation in James, Conrad, and Ford*. Ithaca, NY: Cornell University Press, 1987.

———. *The Phenomenology of Henry James*. Chapel Hill: University of North Carolina Press, 1983.

Auerbach, Nina. *Woman and the Demon: The Life of a Victorian Myth*. Cambridge: Harvard University Press, 1982.

Bataille, Georges. *Death and Sensuality*. New York: Walker, 1962.

Bettelheim, Bruno. *The Uses of Enchantment: The Meaning and Importance of Fairy Tales*. New York: Knopf, 1976.

Bloom, Harold. *The Anxiety of Influence: A Theory of Poetry*. London: Oxford University Press, 1975.

———. *Deconstruction and Criticism*. New York: Continuum, 1979.

———. *The Breaking of the Vessels*. Chicago: University of Chicago Press, 1982.

———. *Map of Misreading*. New York: Oxford University Press, 1975.

Briggs, Asa. *Victorian People: A Reassessment of Persons and Themes, 1851–1867*. 1955. Reprint. Chicago: University of Chicago Press, 1970.

Clawson, Mary Ann. "Nineteenth-Century Women's Auxiliaries and Fraternal Orders." *Signs* 12, no. 1 (Autumn 1986): 40–62.

Culler, Jonathan. *Framing the Sign: Criticism and Its Institutions*. Norman: University of Oklahoma Press, 1989.

Derrida, Jacques. *Glas*. translated by John P. Leavey, Jr., and Richard Rand. Lincoln: University of Nebraska Press, 1986.

————. *L'ecriture et la difference.* 1967. Reprint. Paris: Editions du Seuil, 1979.

————. *Of Grammatology.* Translated by G. C. Spivak. Baltimore, MD: Johns Hopkins University Press, 1974.

Dulac, Edmund. *Edmund Dulac's Fairy-Book: Fairy Tales of the Allied Nations.* 1915. Reprint. New York: Portland House, 1988.

During, Simon. "The Strange Case of Monomania: Patriarchy in Literature, Murder in *Middlemarch,* Drowning in *Daniel Deronda.*" *Representations* no. 23 (Summer 1988): 86–105.

Ellis, John M. *Against Deconstruction.* Princeton: Princeton University Press, 1989.

————. *The Theory of Literary Criticism: A Logical Analysis.* Berkeley: University of California Press, 1974.

Fish, Stanley. *Self-Consuming Artifacts.* Berkeley: University of California Press, 1972.

Flax, Jane. "Postmodernism and Gender Relations in Feminist Theory." *Signs* 12, no. 4 (Summer 1987): 621–44.

Fortin, Nina E., and Gaye Tuckman. *Edging Women Out: Victorian Novelists, Publishers, and Social Change.* New Haven: Yale University Press, 1989.

Ford, George H. *Victorian Fiction: A Second Guide to Research.* New York: Modern Language Association of America, 1978.

Foucault, Michel. "What Is an Author." *Textual Strategies: Perpectives in Structuralist Criticism.* Edited by J. V. Harari. Ithaca, NY: Cornell University Press, 1979, Pp. 141–60.

Freud, Sigmund. *Complete Works.* The Standard Edition. Translated by James Strachey. London: Hogarth Press, 1953.

————. *Dora: An Analysis of a Case of Hysteria.* New York: Collier Books, 1963

————. *Delusion and Dream: And Other Essays.* Edited by Philip Rieff. Boston: Beacon Press, 1956.

————. *A General Introduction to Psychoanalysis.* Joan Riviere. New York: Simon and Schuster, 1953.

————. *The Interpretation of Dreams.* Translated by James Strachey. New York: Basic Books, 1955.

————. *Three Case Histories.* New York: Collier Books, 1963.

Froula, Christine. "The Daughter's Seduction: Sexual Violence and Literary History." *Signs* 11, no. 4 (Summer 1986): 621–45.

Fussell, Paul. *The Great War and Modern Memory.* London: Oxford University Press, 1975.

————. *Thank God for the Atom Bomb and Other Essays.* New York: Summit Books, 1988.

Gadamer, Hans-Georg. *Philosophical Hermeneutics.* Translated by David E. Linge. Berkeley: University of California Press, 1976.

————. *Truth and Method.* Translated anon. New York: Seabury, 1975.

Harari, J. V., ed. *Textual Strategies: Perspectives in Structuralist Criticism.* Ithaca, NY: Cornell University Press, 1979.

Harding, Sandra. "The Instability of the Analytical Categories of Feminist Theory." *Signs* 11, no. 4 (Summer 1986): 645–65.

Hardy, Barbara. *Forms of Feeling in Victorian Fiction.* Ohio: Ohio University Press, 1985.

Hawkesworth, Mary E. "Knowers, Knowing, Known: Feminist Theory and Claims of Truth." *Signs* 14, no. 3 (Spring 1989): 533–58.

Heidegger, Martin. *Basic Writings.* Edited by David F. Krell. New York: Harper and Row, 1977.

————. *Being and Time.* New York: Harper and Row, 1962.

————. *Poetry, Language, Thought.* Translated by Albert Hofstadter. New York: Harper and Row, 1971.

Hirsch, Donald E. *Validity in Interpretation.* New Haven: Yale University Press, 1967.

Holstein, Suzy Clarkson. "A 'Root Deeper than All Change': The Daughter's Longing in the Victorian Novel." *Victorian Newsletter* no. 75 (Spring 1989): 20–28.

Houghton, Walter. *The Victorian Frame of Mind.* New Haven: Yale University Press, 1957.

Husserl, Edmund. *Cartesian Meditations: An Introduction to Phenomenology.* Translated by Dorian Cairns. The Hague: Martinus Nijhoff, 1977.

Ingarden, Roman. *The Literary Work of Art.* Translated by George C. Grabowicz. Evanston, IL: Northwestern University Press, 1973.

Iser, Wolfgang. *The Act of Reading: A Theory of Aesthetic Response.* Baltimore: Johns Hopkins University Press, 1979.

———. *The Implied Reader: Patterns of Communication in Prose Fiction from Bunyan to Beckett.* Baltimore: Johns Hopkins University Press, 1974.

Jameson, Frederic. *The Political Unconscious: Narrative as a Socially Symbolic Act.* Ithaca, NY: Cornell University Press, 1981.

Kant, Immanuel. *Critique of Judgment.* Translated by James C. Meredith. New York: Random House, 1949.

Kierkegaard, Soren. *The Concept of Dread.* Translated by Walter Lowrie. Princeton: Princeton University Press, 1970.

———. *Fear and Trembling: A Dialectical Lyric.* Translated by Walter Lowrie. Princeton: Princeton University Press, 1941.

Knoepflmacher, U. C. "The Balancing of Child and Adult: An Approach to Victorian Fantasies for Children." *Nineteenth-Century Fiction* 37, no. 4 (March 1983): 497–530.

Kucich, John. "Narrative Theory as History: A Review of Problems in Victorian Fiction Studies." *Victorian Studies*, 28, no. 4 (Summer 1985): 657–75.

Lentricchia, Frank. *After the New Criticism.* Chicago: University of Chicago Press, 1980.

Makinnon, Catherine A. "Feminism, Marxism, Method, and the State: An Agenda for Theory." *Signs* 7 (1982): 515–44.

Moynihan, Robert, ed. *A Recent Imagining: Interviews with Harold Bloom, Geoffrey Hartman, J. Hillis Miller, Paul De Man.* Hamden, CT: Archer Books, 1986.

Nelson, Barbara J. "Women's Poverty and Woman's Citizenship: Some Political Consequences of Economic Marginality." *Signs* 10, no. 2 (Winter 1984): 209–32.

Offen, Karen. "Defining Feminism: A Comparative Historical Approach." *Signs* 14, no. 1 (Autumn 1988): 119–58.

Orgel, Stephen. "The Authentic Shakespeare." *Representations* no. 21 (Winter 1988): 1–27.

Phelan, James. *Reading People, Reading Plots: Character, Progression, and the Interpretation of Narrative.* Chicago: University of Chicago Press, 1989.

Pike, E. Royston, ed. *Golden Times: Human Documents of the Victorian Age.* New York: Schocken Books, 1972.

Reagan, Charles S., and David Stewart, eds. *The Philosophy of Paul Ricoeur.* Boston: Beacon Press, 1978.

Reed, John R. "A Friend to Mammon: Speculation in Victorian Literature." *Victorian Studies* 27, no. 2 (Winter 1984): 179–203.

Ricoeur, Paul. *Freud and Philosophy.* Translated by Denis Savage. New Haven, CT: Yale University Press, 1970.

Sartre, Jean-Paul. *Literature and Existentialism.* Translated by Bernard Frechtman. Secaucus, NJ: The Citadel Press, 1972.

Showalter, Elaine. "Looking Forward: American Feminists, Victorian Sages." *Victorian Newsletter* no. 65 (Spring 1984): 6–10 .

Showalter, Elaine, ed. *The New Feminist Criticism.* New York: Pantheon Books, 1985.

Smith, Barbara Herrnstein. *Contingencies of Value: Alternative Perspectives for Critical Theory.* Cambridge: Harvard University Press, 1989.

————. *On the Margins of Discourse: The Relation of Literature to Language.* Chicago: University of Chicago Press, 1978.

Smith, Ruth L., and Deborah M. Valenze. "Mutuality and Marginality: Liberal Moral Theory and Working-Class Women in Nineteenth-Century England." *Signs* 13, no. 2 (Winter 1988): 277–99.

Spitzer, Leo. *Linguistics and Literary History.* Princeton: Princeton University Press, 1948.

Stevenson, Lionel, ed. *Victorian Fiction—A Guide to Research.* Cambridge: Harvard University Press, 1964.

Tompkins, Jane P. *Sensational Designs: The Cultural Works of American Fiction, 1790–1860.* New York: Oxford University Press, 1986.

Torgounick, Marianna. "Closure and the Victorian Novel, 1986." *Victorian Newsletter* no. 71 (Spring 1987): 4–7.

Trodd, Anthea. "The Policeman and the Lady: Significant Encounters in Mid-Victorian Fiction." *Victorian Studies* 27, no. 4 (Summer 1984): 435–61.

Walsh, Susan A. "Darling Mothers, Devilish Queens: The Divided Women in Victorian Fantasy." *Victorian Newsletter* no. 72 (Fall 1987): 32–36.

Welsh, Alexander. "The Evidence of Things Not Seen: Justice Stephen and Bishop Butler." *Representations* no. 22 (Spring 1988): 60–89.

Wittgenstein, Ludwig. *The Blue and Brown Books.* New York: Harper and Row, 1958.

————. *Lectures and Conversations on Aesthetics, Psychology and Religious Belief.* Edited by Cyril Barrett. Berkeley: University of California Press, 1978.

————. *On Certainty.* 1969. Reprint. Edited by G. E. M. Anscombe and G. H. von Wright. New York: Harper and Row, 1972.

————. *Philosophical Grammar.* 1974. Reprint. Edited by Rush Rhees. Berkeley: University of California Press, 1978.

————. *Philosophical Investigations.* Translated by G. E. M. Anscombe. New York: Macmillan, 1958.

————. *Remarks on Colour.* Edited by G. E. M. Anscombe. Berkeley: University of California Press, 1977.

————. *Zettel.* 1967. Reprint. Edited by G. E. M. Anscombe and G. H. von Wright. Berkeley: University of California Press, 1970.

Index

Page numbers with illustrations appear in *boldface italics*.